Citizenship

Series Editor: Cara Acred

Volume 312

Independence Educational Publishers

First published by Independence Educational Publishers

The Studio, High Green

Great Shelford

Cambridge CB22 5EG

England

© Independence 2017

Copyright

Photocopy licence

ISBN-13: 978 1 86168 762 3

Printed in Great Britain

Zenith Print Group

Contents

Introduction

Citizenship is Volume 312 in the **ISSUES** series. The aim of the series is to offer current, diverse information about important issues in our world, from a UK perspective.

ABOUT TITLE

What does it mean to be a UK citizen? What does it mean to be a global citizen? What does it mean to be a citizen of the EU, and what does our post-Brexit future look like? This book explores all of these topics, and more. It also considers ways in which young people can become 'good' or 'active' citizens, through activities such as volunteering and involvement in politics, and encourages engagement in the topic of national identity.

OUR SOURCES

Titles in the **ISSUES** series are designed to function as educational resource books, providing a balanced overview of a specific subject.

The information in our books is comprised of facts, articles and opinions from many different sources, including:

⇨ Newspaper reports and opinion pieces

⇨ Website factsheets

⇨ Magazine and journal articles

⇨ Statistics and surveys

⇨ Government reports

⇨ Literature from special interest groups.

A NOTE ON CRITICAL EVALUATION

Because the information reprinted here is from a number of different sources, readers should bear in mind the origin of the text and whether the source is likely to have a particular bias when presenting information (or when conducting their research). It is hoped that, as you read about the many aspects of the issues explored in this book, you will critically evaluate the information presented.

It is important that you decide whether you are being presented with facts or opinions. Does the writer give a biased or unbiased report? If an opinion is being expressed, do you agree with the writer? Is there potential bias to the 'facts' or statistics behind an article?

ASSIGNMENTS

In the back of this book, you will find a selection of assignments designed to help you engage with the articles you have been reading and to explore your own opinions. Some tasks will take longer than others and there is a mixture of design, writing and research-based activities that you can complete alone or in a group.

Useful weblinks

www.britishfuture.org

www.bsa.ac.uk

www.centreonconstitutionalchange.ac.uk

www.theconversation.com

www.crickcentre.org

GOV.UK.

www.theguardian.com

www.ipsos-mori.com

www.migrationobservatory.ox.ac.uk

www.natcen.ac.uk

parliament.uk.

researchbriefings.parliament.uk

www.responsiblecitizen.co.uk

www.ukandeu.ac.uk

www.weforum.org

www.yougov.co.uk

FURTHER RESEARCH

At the end of each article we have listed its source and a website that you can visit if you would like to conduct your own research. Please remember to critically evaluate any sources that you consult and consider whether the information you are viewing is accurate and unbiased.

National identity

The concept of national identity

There are two widely accepted conceptions of nationality: 'ethnic' and 'civic', both of which are linked to the development of nations and states in Europe. The civic conception of nationalism helps explain the development of nations in states that had already emerged as political and geographical units (for example, France). As such, the nation was defined as the totality of people living within the boundaries of that state and abiding by its laws. This is why in the French conception of nationalism the words 'nationality' and 'citizenship' denote the same thing: belonging to the French state. Indeed, in the civic conception of nationalism, the nation and the citizenry are one and the same, which is why such states are often referred to as nation states. Consequently, when we think of national identity in civic terms, we think of an inclusive form of identity: a person associates themselves with the citizenry and the political and

legal institutions of the state. His or her identity is defined by attachment to the state as embodied by its institutions and rules and not by traditions, language or religion. Conversely, when we think of ethnic nationalism, traditions, language, religion and ancestry are precisely the things that matter. As opposed to the civic nation, the ethnic conception of nationalism came into existence in Germany and Eastern Europe as a response of communities in highly fragmented societies (such as the Austro-Hungarian empire) searching to define themselves. While civic nationalism emerged after, and as a response to, the emergence of a physical state, ethnic nationalism emerged and solidified culturally distinct communities who were looking to form their own state. This is why in nation states where the ethnic conception of nationalism dominates there is a clear distinction between citizenship and nationality. Citizenship denotes a person's legal status vis-à-vis

the state; nationality denotes his or her intrinsic identity. Ethnic national identity is characterised by an attachment to one's ancestry, tradition, culture and language – and not necessarily to the state a person was born and lives in. This is why an ethnic national identity is exclusive: if you are not born into it, you cannot acquire it (Ignatieff, 1995).

This discussion assumes a very clear distinction between the two types of national identity. While this is accurate in certain circumstance and some states neatly fit into one or other category (for example, France and Germany), the picture in the UK is more complicated. Britishness is described as being a 'fuzzy' concept that cannot be readily placed into either of these two buckets. As such, a matrix is proposed within which these two types of national identity intersect with one another, producing four possible types of national identity.

Defining British identity

We assessed how people think of national identity by asking the following questions as part of the 1995, 2003 and 2013 British Social Attitudes surveys:

Some people say that the following things are important for being truly British. Others say that they are not important. How important do you think each of the following is?

⇨   To have been born in Britain

⇨   To have British citizenship

⇨   To have lived in Britain for most of one's life

⇨   To be able to speak English

⇨   To be a Christian

⇨   To respect Britain's political institutions and laws

⇨   To feel British

⇨   To have British ancestry

We asked an additional question to assess

the extent to which shared customs and traditions matter:

Now we would like to ask a few questions about minority groups in Britain. How much do you agree or disagree with the following statement? It is impossible for people who do not share Britain's customs and traditions to become fully British.

Of the nine attributes we asked about, six are seen as "very" or "fairly" important by around three-quarters of people or more. The most important factor is being able to speak English (which 95 per cent think is important), followed by having British citizenship and respecting Britain's political institutions and laws (both 85 per cent). Around three-quarters think being born in Britain is important, but only half that having British ancestry matters. It is notable that only a quarter think that being Christian is important for being "truly British".

If we look at the data from a historical perspective, it is clear that, despite little change between 1995 and 2003, there have been some major shifts since then. In particular, the perceived importance of being able to speak English has increased by nearly ten percentage points. There has also been an increase in the proportion who think it important that someone has lived for most of their life in Britain, up from 69 per cent in 2003 to 77 per cent now.

To understand how these results correspond to the two identity dimensions we mentioned earlier (ethnic versus civic) we used a technique called factor analysis. The results of this analysis [...] show that responses [...] do indeed divide into two different dimensions, which correspond well with the differences between ethnic and civic conceptions of national identity.

We then calculated an ethnic identity score and a civic identity score for each respondent, based on how they had answered these questions. In each case, the closer the score is to five, the more weight that person puts on the relevant dimension of national identity, and the closer it is to 0, the less weight. The results show that the vast majority of Britons do not see whether or not someone is "truly British" as being down to solely civic or ethnic criteria – instead, many see both as playing a role. Another, smaller, group have an entirely civic view of national identity. Almost nobody has an entirely ethnic view. Finally, there is also evidence of a group whose views about national identity have neither an ethnic nor a civic component.

The majority of people (nearly two-thirds) attach importance to both ethnic and civic aspects of national identity while about one-third tend to think of national identity only in civic terms. Six per cent do not appear to think of national identity in either ethnic or civic terms. Comparing these findings with those from earlier years shows considerable continuity, although there is the hint of a small increase in the proportion of the population with a civic notion of national identity, from 23 per cent in 1995 to 34 per cent in 2003 and 31 per cent in 2013. There has also been a small change in the proportion who think that both civic and ethnic aspects of national identity matter: after a four percentage point dip between 1995 and 2003, by 2013 this proportion had returned to its 1995 level of 63 per cent.

Of course, these overall findings are likely to mask considerable differences between particular groups. An obvious starting point here is age; we know from earlier work that there are clear age differences in national pride, with younger groups being less likely than older ones to express pride in being British (Young, 2014). We explore this in Table 4.5. However, rather than focusing on age, we examine the views of specific generations as there are strong reasons to suspect that their different experiences during their formative years (particularly in terms of their exposure to war and conflict) will have had an impact on the way they think about Britain and British identity.

To do this we pooled together our 2003 and 2013 findings (to increase the sample size available for analysis) and then allocated people into one of three different generational groups: those born before 1945; those born between 1945 and 1964; and those born after 1964. The results show that there are indeed considerable generational differences; nearly nine in ten of the pre-1945 generation have a civic and ethnic view of British national identity, but the same is only true of six in ten of those born between 1945 and 1964, falling to five in ten among the youngest generation. Conversely, while 40 per cent of those born after 1964 have a view of British national identity based only on civic factors, this is true of just 13 per cent of those born before 1945.

These findings suggest that, over time, the importance attached to ascribed ethnic factors in thinking about national identity may well decline, as older generations die out and are replaced by generations who are less likely to think of Britishness as dependent on factors such as birth, ancestry and sharing customs and traditions.

2014

⇨ The above information is reprinted with kind permission from NatCen Social Research. Please visit www.bsa.natcen.ac.uk for further information.

Table 4.5 Distribution of conceptions of national identity, by generation, 2003 and 2013			
	Born pre- 1945	Born 1945–1964	Born post- 1964
	%	%	%
Civic and ethnic	86	61	50
Only civic	13	33	40
Neither civic nor ethnic	2	5	10
Weighted base	*341*	*591*	*737*
Unweighted base	*408*	*588*	*663*

Types of British nationality

Overview

There are six different types of British nationality. These are:

⇨ British citizenship

⇨ British overseas territories citizen

⇨ British overseas citizen

⇨ British subject

⇨ British national (overseas)

⇨ British protected person.

British citizenship

You can live and work in the UK free of any immigration controls if you're a British citizen – check if you're a British citizen if you're not sure.

You may be able to apply to register as a British citizen if you have another type of British nationality.

If you were born in the UK before 1 January 1983

You became a British citizen on 1 January 1983 if both of the following apply:

⇨ you were a citizen of the UK and Colonies

⇨ you had the 'right of abode' in the UK

'Right of abode' means you:

⇨ are entirely free from UK Immigration Control and don't need permission from an Immigration Officer to enter the UK

⇨ can live and work in the UK without restriction.

This includes people who:

⇨ were born in the UK

⇨ were born in a British colony and had the right of abode in the UK

⇨ have been naturalised in the UK

⇨ had registered as a citizen of the UK and Colonies

⇨ could prove legitimate descent from a father to whom one of these applies.

If you were born in the UK on or after 1 January 1983

You don't automatically get British citizenship if you were born in the UK.

If you were born on or after 1 January 1983, you'll be a British citizen if your mother or father was either:

⇨ a British citizen when you were born

⇨ 'settled' in the UK when you were born.

In most cases you'll be a British citizen if your mother or father was born in the UK or naturalised there at the time of your birth.

If you were born before July 2006, your father's British nationality will normally only pass to you if he was married to your mother at the time of your birth.

If your circumstances are more complicated, you can get more information about British citizenship.

Born outside the UK

You might qualify for British citizenship depending on your circumstances – check if you're a British citizen if you're not sure.

If you're a foreign national or Commonwealth citizen, you don't automatically gain citizenship just because you live in the UK.

British overseas territories citizen

British overseas territories citizenship was called 'British dependent territories citizenship' before 26 February 2002.

If you were born before 1 January 1983

You became a British overseas territories citizen on 1 January 1983 if both of these applied:

⇨ you were a citizen of the United Kingdom and Colonies on 31 December 1982

⇨ you had connections with a British overseas territory because you, your parents or your grandparents were born, registered or naturalised in that British overseas territory.

You also became a British overseas territories citizen if you were a woman married to a man who became a British overseas territories citizen on 1 January 1983.

If you were born on or after 1 January 1983

You're a British overseas territories citizen if both the following apply:

⇨ you were born in a British overseas territory

⇨ at the time of your birth one of your parents was a British overseas territories citizen or legally settled in a British overseas territory.

You're also a British overseas territories citizen if one of the following applies:

⇨ you were adopted in an overseas territory by a British overseas territories citizen

⇨ you were born outside the overseas territory to a parent who gained British overseas territories citizenship in their own right (known as 'otherwise than by descent')

Rights as a British overseas territories citizen

You can:

⇨ hold a British passport

⇨ get consular assistance and protection from UK diplomatic posts.

Unless you're also a British citizen:

⇨ you're still subject to immigration controls – you don't have the automatic right to live or work in the UK

⇨ you aren't considered a UK national by the European Union (EU).

British citizenship

You automatically became a British citizen on 21 May 2002 if your British overseas territories citizenship was gained by connection with a qualifying territory.

The qualifying territories are:

⇨ Anguilla

⇨ Bermuda

- ⇨ British Antarctic Territory
- ⇨ British Indian Ocean Territory
- ⇨ British Virgin Islands
- ⇨ Cayman Islands
- ⇨ Falkland Islands
- ⇨ Gibraltar
- ⇨ Montserrat
- ⇨ Pitcairn Islands
- ⇨ Saint Helena, Ascension and Tristan da Cunha
- ⇨ South Georgia and the South Sandwich Islands
- ⇨ Turks and Caicos Islands.

Register as a British citizen

You may be able to register as a British citizen if you became a British overseas territories citizen after 21 May 2002 and meet certain conditions.

British overseas citizen

You became a British overseas citizen on 1 January 1983 if both of these applied:

- ⇨ you were a citizen of the United Kingdom and Colonies on 31 December 1982
- ⇨ you didn't become either a British citizen or a British overseas territories citizen on 1 January 1983

Hong Kong

If you were a British overseas territories citizen only because of your connection with Hong Kong you lost that citizenship on 30 June 1997 when sovereignty returned to China.

However, you became a British overseas citizen if either:

- ⇨ you had no other nationality and would have become stateless
- ⇨ you were born on or after 1 July 1997 and would have been born stateless if one of your parents was a British national (overseas) or British overseas citizen when you were born

Rights as a British overseas citizen

You can:

- ⇨ hold a British passport
- ⇨ get consular assistance and

protection from UK diplomatic posts.

Unless you're also a British citizen:

- ⇨ you're still subject to immigration controls – you don't have the automatic right to live or work in the UK
- ⇨ you aren't considered a UK national by the European Union (EU).

Become a British overseas citizen

You can only apply to become a British overseas citizen in limited circumstances.

Stateless people

You may be able to register as a British overseas citizen if you're stateless (not recognised by any country as having a nationality) and both of these apply:

- ⇨ you were born in the UK or an overseas territory
- ⇨ one of your parents is a British overseas citizen.

You may also be able to register if you're stateless and all of these apply:

- ⇨ you were born outside the UK and qualifying territories
- ⇨ one of your parents is a British overseas citizen
- ⇨ you've lived in the UK or an overseas territory for three years or more.

You have to fill in different forms depending on whether you were:

- ⇨ born before 1 January 1983 - read the guidance and fill in Form S1
- ⇨ born on or after 1 January 1983 – read the guidance and fill in Form S2.

Children

A child under 18 can be registered as a British overseas citizen in special circumstances.

British subject

Until 1949, nearly everyone with a close connection to the United Kingdom was called a 'British subject'.

All citizens of Commonwealth countries were British subjects until January 1983.

Since 1983, very few people have qualified as British subjects.

Who is a British subject

You became a British subject on 1 January 1983 if, until then, you were either:

- ⇨ a British subject without citizenship, which means you were a British subject on 31 December 1948 who didn't become a citizen of the UK and Colonies, a Commonwealth country, Pakistan or the Republic of Ireland
- ⇨ a person who had been a citizen of the Republic of Ireland on 31 December 1948 and had made a claim to remain a British subject.

You also became a British subject on 1 January 1983 if you were a woman who registered as a British subject on the basis of your marriage to a man in one of these categories.

Republic of Ireland citizens

You're a British subject if you were a citizen of the Republic of Ireland on 31 December 1948 and made a claim to remain a British subject.

If you didn't make a claim to remain a British subject you can apply to the Home Secretary to become a British subject if either:

- ⇨ you've been in Crown service for the UK Government
- ⇨ you're associated with the UK or a British overseas territory by descent, residence or another way.

You can do this by applying for a British subject passport.

Children of British subjects

British subjects can't normally pass on that status to their children if the children were born after 1 January 1983.

However, a child may be a British subject if they were born on or after 1 January 1983 in the UK or a British overseas territory and all the following apply when they are born:

- ⇨ one of their parents is a British subject
- ⇨ neither parent is a British citizen, British overseas territories citizen or British overseas citizen
- ⇨ they would be stateless without British subject status.

Rights as a British subject

You can:

⇨ hold a British passport

⇨ get consular assistance and protection from UK diplomatic posts.

However, you:

⇨ are usually subject to immigration controls and don't have the automatic right to live or work in the UK (there are only rare exceptions to this)

⇨ aren't considered a UK national by the European Union (EU).

Becoming a British subject

Stateless people

You may sometimes be able to register as a British subject if:

⇨ you're stateless (not recognised by any country as having a nationality)

⇨ you were born outside the UK or British overseas territories on or after 1 January 1983.

You must meet certain conditions. Read the guidance notes before you apply using Form S2.

Children

A child under 18 can be registered as a British subject in special circumstances.

Becoming a citizen of another country

Since 1 January 1983 anyone gaining citizenship of any other country can't be a British subject, unless they're also a citizen of the Republic of Ireland.

23 September 2016

⇨ The above information is reprinted with kind permission from GOV.UK.

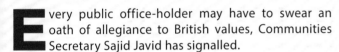

British values oath proposed by Sajid Javid

By Chris York

Every public office-holder may have to swear an oath of allegiance to British values, Communities Secretary Sajid Javid has signalled.

The loyalty pledge would be expected to cover elected officials, civil servants and council workers.

Javid's proposal comes in response to a report on social cohesion by Dame Louise Casey, which warned some sections of society did not accept British values such as tolerance.

He said he was "drawn" to Dame Louise's recommendation to bring in an oath of allegiance because it was impossible for people to play a "positive role" in public life unless they accepted basic values like democracy and equality.

Writing in *The Sunday Times*, Mr Javid said: "If we are going to challenge such attitudes, civic and political leaders have to lead by example.

"We can't expect new arrivals to embrace British values if those of us who are already here don't do so ourselves, and such an oath would go a long way to making that happen."

Mr Javid said his aim was not to create a "government-approved one size fits all identity" where everybody listens to the Last Night of the Proms, but "without common building blocks of our society, you'll struggle to play a positive role in British life".

The oath could include phrases such as "tolerating the views of others even if you disagree with them", as well as "believing in freedom of speech, freedom of religion, freedom from abuse... a belief in equality, democracy and the democratic process" and "respect for the law, even if you think the law is an ass".

Mr Javid also wants all migrants to swear an oath of allegiance, not just those seeking UK citizenship, *The Sunday Times* said.

Dame Louise's report warned the country was becoming more divided as it became more diverse and highlighted that in some communities women were the subject of "abuse and unequal treatment of women enacted in the name of cultural or religious values".

"Every public office-holder may have to swear an oath of allegiance to British values"

In her report she acknowledged that elements would be "hard to read", particularly for Muslim communities which already felt under pressure, but she said the country had to face up to "uncomfortable" problems.

The review recommended that schoolchildren should be taught "British values" of tolerance, democracy and respect to help bind communities together amid growing "ethnic segregation".

The review was originally commissioned by then prime minister David Cameron in 2015 as part of a wider strategy to tackle the "poison" of Islamic extremism.

It found that while Britain had benefited hugely from immigration and the increased ethnic and religious diversity it had brought, there had not been sufficient emphasis on integration.

18 December 2016

⇨ The above information is reprinted with kind permission from The Huffington Post UK. Please visit www.huffingtonpost.co.uk for further information.

Naturalisation as a British citizen: concepts and trends

This briefing gives details about how many foreign citizens acquire British citizenship every year, their demographic characteristics, and the various bases for their grants of British citizenship.

By Dr Scott Blinder

Citizenship grants per year more than doubled from 2000 to 2013 but fell considerably in 2014 and 2015

In 2015, 118,100 foreign citizens naturalised as British citizens. This is down more than 40% from 2013, when citizenship grants reached almost 208,000, the largest annual number since records began in 1962. From 2009 to 2013, citizenship grants averaged 195,800 per year.

"Nationals of EU countries made up only 11% of citizenship grants in 2015"

According to the Home Office (2014), the 2013 peak in citizenship grants followed an increase in applications in advance of changes to language requirements, while lower numbers of grants in 2014 were at least in part due to the shifting of resources from UK Visas and Immigration to HM Passport Office. The number of decisions made on citizenship applications in 2015 did not increase in line with an increase in the number of applications submitted (applications increased by about 23,700 or 18% from 2014 to 2015), suggesting that the declining trend in citizenship grants may end in 2016 as these applications are processed.

Lower numbers of citizenship applications in recent years are also consistent with recent decreases in grants of settlement/indefinite leave to remain (from 241,200 in 2010 to 129,800 in 2012 and 154,700 in 2013), which will have reduced the pool of people newly eligible to apply for citizenship.

The number of accepted and rejected citizenship applications is affected by policy and administrative changes

The acceptance rate for naturalisation applications was increasing until 2013, when 3.4% of applications ended in refusal or withdrawal. This was down from 3.9% in 2010, 9.3% as recently as 2005, and at least 10% for most of the 1990s. The increased acceptance rates up to 2010 were at least partially the result of new application checking services that catch incomplete or inadequate applications before they are filed (Home Office, 2010: 10). In 2014, 4.7% of applications were refused rising to 8.6% in 2015. According to the Home Office (2016), this decline in the grant rate can be attributed to the introduction of "enhanced checks on cases requiring higher levels of assurance" in April 2015.

The trend in naturalisations has several notable spikes that can be explained as the result of changes to law or administrative procedures. In chronological order: 1974–1975 saw an increase in grants to Pakistanis following the Pakistan Act of 1973 (which created a temporary window for Pakistani nationals to register as Citizens of the United Kingdom and Colonies, after which naturalisation would be required as for non-commonwealth nationals). Next, the increase in 1989 comes from the opening of a new application processing centre in Liverpool, increasing administrative capacity. Finally, increases in grants through registration since 2003 may reflect new provisions in the Nationality, Immigration and Asylum Act 2002 (Home Office, 2010: Table A notes).

The introduction of the Life in the UK test and more stringent English language requirements in 2004 does not seem to have changed the increasing trend in naturalisations until 2013. It is possible that there would have been more naturalisations without these new requirements (including not only the newly-required knowledge and skill tests but also the fees required to prepare for and take them). Further, the language and knowledge requirements would seem to pose a greater burden on nationals of poorer, less educated and non-English-speaking countries (Ryan 2008), and may have deterred applications among nationals of such countries.

Residency, marriage and children are the three main grounds for citizenship grants

As noted above, British citizenship grants are divided among three main categories: migrants fulfilling the five-year residency requirement, spouses and civil partners of British citizens, and underage children being registered as citizens. About half of grants overall come from residency requirements (51% in 2015). The two family routes (marriage/civil partnership and children) account for slightly less than half combined (marriage/civil partnership made up 21% in 2015; children made up 24% in 2015). The remaining 4% were "other" bases for citizenship, including, for example, transfers from British overseas territories citizenship to full citizenship status.

Each of the main pathways to naturalisation (residence, marriage and registration of minor children) grew in numbers from 2000 to 2013 albeit with a temporary decrease in 2008. The decline in citizenship grants in 2014 also took place across all of three main categories.

Residence-related grants increased the most over the 2000s, both in number and in percentage terms. Grants from residence increased from 35,000 in 2000 to 113,300 in 2013, before falling to 62,500 in 2014 and 60,800 in 2015. Naturalisation through marriage almost doubled in the decade of the 2000s, from 27,400 in 2000 to 52,600 in 2009 but then decreased to 24,400 in 2015. Grants to minor children increased from 19,200 in 2000 to a peak of 48,600 in 2010, and stood at 28,700 in 2015. Since 2000 residence-related grants have grown from 43% of naturalisations in 2000 to 51% in 2015, while marriage-based grants declined from 33% to 20% in the same period. Minor children

registrations constituted 23% in 2000 and 24% in 2015. "Other" categories fluctuated between 1% and 5%.

89% of grants of citizenship in 2015 were to non-EU nationals

The largest groups of newly naturalised UK citizens in 2015 had prior citizenship from India, Pakistan, Nigeria, and South Africa. Asian nations contributed the most to growth in naturalisations over time. African nationals also contributed heavily to the growth in naturalisations in the 2000s. Nigeria, South Africa, Zimbabwe, and Ghana ranked among the top ten prior nationalities of new UK citizens in 2015.

Nationals of EU countries made up only 11% of citizenship grants in 2015, despite their significant contribution to overall UK migration over the past decade. Data on naturalisations of EU citizens for 2016 – before and after the UK voted to leave the European Union – will become available in May 2017.

Europe and the Middle East grew as sources of naturalising British citizens until 2013, while only the Americas declined as a source region for naturalisations during this period. Naturalisations among citizens of countries that joined the EU in 2004 are a small share of total grants of citizenship (5% in 2015), but increased sharply from 2009 onwards as people arriving in the mid-2000s began to be eligible to naturalise. The number of citizens of accession (A8) countries rose from 869 in 2009 to just under 8,300 in 2013. Since then it has dropped to 5,800 in 2015.

Grants of citizenship to nationals of North and South American countries averaged 21,100 annually between 1983 and 1989 before dropping to only 4,900 annually in the 1990s and 10,800 annually from 2000 to 2015.

Legal barriers, language and integration, and poverty in origin country affect naturalisation rates

Naturalisation reflects both legal requirements and a personal choice on the part of a foreign national to apply

to become British. Therefore, one might expect that naturalisation is more likely when there are few legal barriers, when naturalisation brings greater benefits, and when naturalising does not mean giving up much of value, such as a previous citizenship. Strands of research have investigated each of these aspects of the determinants of naturalisation rates.

First, naturalisation rates are indeed lower in nations that impose more legal requirements for acquiring citizenship. Traditionally, nations have been categorised as following one of two logics of citizenship: jus soli (literally 'right of soil') where citizenship comes from being born in the country, and *jus sanguinis* (literally 'right of blood') where citizenship comes from parents' citizenship and in-country birth does not confer citizenship. Contemporary citizenship law in many nations blends the two logics in varying proportions.

Overall, British citizenship law is more open to naturalisation than traditional jus sanguinis nations such as Germany. However, although it may be viewed as the original jus soli country, it is now less open than other traditional jus soli nations such as the USA and Canada. In a comprehensive comparative study, Janoski (2010) identifies as many as 12 requirements that countries may impose; British citizenship law now includes many from this list (Sawyer 2009).

These include requirements of good conduct, language skills, efforts toward cultural integration (measured in the form of the Life in the UK test), years of residency, and navigation of complex and expensive application procedures.

From 2002 to 2015, the majority of refusals to grant citizenship were because of a failure to meet either the 'good character' requirement or the residence requirement. The 'good character' requirement accounts for an increasing number of rejected applications for naturalisation, rising to 42% of all refusals in 2015 (from 10% to 13% in the years immediately preceding legal changes to this requirement in 2008). Failure to demonstrate language proficiency or knowledge of life in the UK comprised 5% of refusals (532 people). The most common reason for refusal was the failure to meet the 'good character' requirement. Refusals due to delays in replying to enquiries from UK Visas and Immigration (UKVI) have risen in recent years – from 423 in 2013 (6%) to 1,251 in 2015 (12%).

On the other hand, British citizenship law does not have many *jus sanguinis* characteristics, making it relatively easy for children born in the UK to non-British parents to be registered for British citizenship. British citizenship law also does not require renunciation of prior citizenships in order to naturalise. (Law in the sending nation is relevant here as well. Zimbabwe, for example, has not permitted dual citizenship, probably lowering naturalisation rates for Zimbabwean migrants to the UK.)

Research on the individual determinants of naturalisation – the ways in which the costs and benefits to individuals determine their likelihood of naturalising – has been conducted mainly in North America and not in the UK (Bloemraad, 2006). A recent European study of naturalisation identifies nine factors associated with higher naturalisation rates. At the individual level, naturalisation is more likely for migrants who speak the destination country's language, who have a parent born in the destination country and who reside longer within it. In addition, people who came from a poor or unstable country or from a former colony of the destination country are more likely to naturalise. Among the second generation (children of migrants), naturalisation seems to be less common among Muslims than among others. In the destination country, the study finds higher naturalisation rates where citizenship law is relatively permissive and where net migration rates are low (Dronkers and Vink, 2010).

For migrants to the UK, the basis for initial entry also partially determines the likelihood of naturalising. Migrants who arrive in the UK with family visas or as skilled or highly-skilled workers (pre-PBS equivalents of Tier 1 and Tier 2 visas) are more likely to naturalise than those with student visas or temporary work visas. Students and temporary workers do not accumulate time toward fulfilling residency requirements unless they change their status to a category that is eligible for naturalisation, for instance through marriage to a British national or by obtaining a visa based on longer term work.

Evidence gaps and limitations

Administrative data on naturalisations provide complete and presumably accurate counts of grants of citizenship by category of eligibility (residence, family or registration). The Home Office compiles figures from a database in which caseworkers enter information about each applicant for naturalisation. Published statistics are generated from this database.

A minority of applications for citizenship are refused; these refusals are also tracked in administrative data, including the reason for rejection. Some of these simply fail to meet straightforward requirements such as length of residence; others reflect more discretionary judgements, such as the 'good character' requirement. In 2008, the Home Office changed its interpretation of the good character clause, making it difficult for people with past criminal convictions to attain citizenship.

Since naturalisation represents a change in relationship between an individual and the Government, trends in naturalisation reflect not only trends in migration but also changes in government policy and administrative practice. Several cases are discussed in this briefing in which a change in policy or administrative practice had noticeable effects on the number of naturalising citizens in a given year or period. However, a crucial limitation is that administrative data on applications, grants and refusals cannot show the number of potential citizenship applications that might be deterred by added requirements. These include the 2004 and 2005 changes requiring a higher standard of English language proficiency and a demonstration of knowledge of life in the UK, and the fees accompanying applications for settlement, naturalisation, and the Life in the UK test. Some research attempts to estimate this deterrent effect (Ryan, 2008), but this requires estimations based on assumptions and cannot be counted straightforwardly in the data. Still, given that some individuals may not feel capable of passing the required language and knowledge tests, and others may have difficulty affording the fees (particularly families, since fees apply to each individual), this deterrence could be an important impact of these policies.

References

Bloemraad, Irene. "Becoming a Citizen in the United States and Canada: Structured Mobilization and Immigrant Political Incorporation." Social Forces 85, no. 2 (2006): 667-695.

Dronkers, Jaap, and Maarten Vink. "Explaining Immigrant Citizenship Status: First and Second Generation Immigrants in Fifteen European States." MPRA Paper No. 26198, Maastricht Research School of Economics of Technology and Organization (METEOR), Maastricht University, 2010. Accessed 9 November 2010. http://mpra.ub.uni-muenchen.de/26198/

Home Office. "British Citizenship Statistics, United Kingdom, 2009." Statistical Bulletin, Home Office, London, 2010.

Home Office. "Immigration Statistics, October to December 2014." London: Home Office, 2015.

Home Office. "User Guide to Home Office Immigration Statistics", updated May 26, 2016.

Janoski, Thomas. The Ironies of Citizenship: Naturalization and Integration in Industrialized Countries. Cambridge: Cambridge University Press, 2010.

Ryan, Bernard. "Integration Requirements: A New Model in Migration Law." Journal of Immigration Asylum and Nationality Law 22, no. 4 (2008): 303-316.

Sawyer, Caroline. "EUDO Citizenship Observatory Country Report: United Kingdom." Florence: European University Institute, 2009. Accessed 9 November 2010. http://cadmus.eui.eu/bitstream/handle/1814/19642/United%20Kingdom2.pdf?sequence=2

Further reading

Brubaker, R. Citizenship and Nationhood in France and Germany. Cambridge, MA: Harvard University Press, 1992.

Yang, P. Q. "Explaining Immigrant Naturalization." International Migration Review 28, no. 3 (1994): 449-477.

8 August 2016

⇨ The above information is reprinted with kind permission from The Migration Observatory. Please visit www.migrationobservatory.ox.ac.uk for further information.

Citizenship in the UK – English, Irish, Scottish or Welsh?

Citizenship in the UK takes on a very different dimension when you factor in the four countries which make up the UK. Although technically, citizens of the UK are known as British, depending on the person whom you ask, you may get the answer of British, English, Scottish, Irish or Welsh. And it entirely depends on the individual as to which answer you will get.

For outsiders, this can seem a little complicated and it is not hard to see why. People from other countries see us play sport at the Olympics as a British team but then also see teams in the football and rugby world cups under the titles of England, Scotland, Wales and Northern Ireland. London is the capital of the country, but Cardiff, Belfast and Edinburgh all assert their own rights to be called capitals as well. And if it was not confusing enough –many people will be offended if called British but they consider themselves Scottish or one of the other nationalities. And the mistake of calling a Scot, Welsh person or Irish person English is one which is even harder to forgive.

Devolution

The issue of devolution is a thorny one and one which complicates the idea of citizenship in the UK even further. The basic idea of devolution was to give the people in each country a say in how issues in that country were run. The Scottish Parliament at the moment has the most independence – which then leads to a notion called the West Lothian question. The West Lothian question basically addresses the situation which arises in the British Government where MPs for constituencies in Scotland can vote on issues affecting people in England – but people and their MPs in England cannot affect what happens in Scotland because their issues are dealt with by the Scottish Parliament.

A United Kingdom?

Whether or not the UK will ever be, or has ever been, truly united, in the hearts and minds of the people who live here is far beyond the scope of this article. It is a fact that many people from Scotland, Wales and Northern Ireland are keen to re-assert their independence from England and feel that England has ruled their countries for too long. But of course, like in every aspect of life, it would be unfair to generalise. Some people are keen to be British and embrace everything that this means. The best tip for outsiders is to always gauge what each individual feels before calling them British, Irish, Scottish or Welsh.

It is not this article's intention to enter into a full-scale debate of what it means to be British and whether devolution is a good thing or not. It is simply to inform the reader of the differences within the UK which mean that being a citizen of the UK and defining nationality in the UK is no cut and dried matter. This is no modern phenomenon. A glance at any Shakespeare historical play will demonstrate that there has been friction between the countries for a very long time. And Hadrian's Wall is testament to the fact that once the Scots in the north and Roman invaders in England were so desperate to be kept separate that such a feat was necessary.

Devolution looks set to continue, with greater powers being granted to the Scottish Parliament and Welsh and Northern Irish assemblies. Where this will leave England and the UK is unclear – but it will be an interesting topic to observe in the future.

23 September 2014

⇨ The above information is reprinted with kind permission from Responsible Citizen. Please visit www.responsiblecitizen.co.uk for further information.

Grants and refusals of citizenship

Year	Total decisions	Total grants	On basis of residence	On basis of marriage	As children	Other grounds	Refusals and withdrawals
to March 2012	181,832	175,267	95,625	34,384	40,512	4,746	6,565
to March 2013	202,742	195,642	107,146	39,663	43,586	5,247	7,100
to March 2014	214,981	206,852	112,380	46,893	43,413	4,166	8,129
to March 2015	121,339	115,540	56,632,	23,533	31,066	4,309	5,799
to March 2016	148,497	134,659	68,415	28,323	32,508	5,413	13,838
Change: latest year	27,158	19,119	11,783	4,790	1,442	1,104	8,039
Percentage change	+22%	+17%	+21%	+20%	+26%	+26%	+139%

Source: National Statistics Citizenship, May 2016

Four years on, are we still the Britain of Danny Boyle's Olympic ceremony?

Can it really be four years since the Olympics came to London? As Rio prepares to light the flame for the next Olympiad, it must be so.

Many of our memories of that summer will be personal. For some, going to the Games themselves: taking my children to watch equestrian events in Greenwich Park, undeterred by the occasional shower, or going out to watch the Olympic torch being carried through our streets.

The biggest moments were shared across the nation: that triple gold medal hour for Mo Farah, Jessica Ennis and Greg Rutherford on the middle Saturday that British athletics will find it difficult ever to surpass. Above all, there was Danny Boyle's opening ceremony – the night when 27 million of us stopped to take in the sweep of our island story of how we, the British, became us, the people we are today. How the Industrial Revolution came to our green and pleasant land; the democratic changes sparked across a century of war and peace; the soundtrack of our lives through these decades of social and technological change.

That Olympic summer surprised people in its ability to bring the country together. Four years on, Britain looks back on it in the wake of a big moment in our post-war political history, a referendum vote that divided us politically over our relationships with Europe, and illuminated many of the economic, social and cultural divisions in Britain today.

The most economically and culturally confident sections of our society have had the unusual experience, on the losing side of the referendum vote, of feeling disoriented and discombobulated by defeat. So Remain voters in the 2012 host city may have watched the *Imagine* documentary on the making of the opening ceremony with a sense of nostalgic reverie, understanding, for the first time, the appeal of the Faragist slogan "I want my country back", albeit looking through the other end of the telescope. Some will feel a sharp sense of dissonance between the resonance of the opening ceremony for them and the referendum outcome.

Indeed, the ceremony's writer Frank Cotterill-Boyce has voiced this sense of dissonance, casting the referendum campaign and its aftermath as a "kind of anti-opening ceremony". Yet the clue is surely there in the numbers: with 27 million Britons tuning in that night, this could not be a story of Britain that belonged to the 16 million who voted for Remain or the 17 million who were part of the 52% majority.

There is plenty in that same opening ceremony story, scripted by Cotterill-Boyce, to resonate with the sense of identity and pride which underpinned the choice of many fellow citizens to vote Leave, too. It was the story of how our country made and remade the modern world, the spectacular forging of those Olympic rings representing the industrial heritage of a country that took pride in making things before the information age arrived, where popular pressure from the suffragettes and the Jarrow marchers extended democracy and created a welfare state.

And this is part of what it means to be a nation. There are histories and cultural meanings that are shared by those who take very different views on the biggest political questions. Our popular national institutions – the monarchy, the NHS or the army, and indeed Team GB itself – belong to those on both sides of the issues that divide us by party or cause when we go to the ballot box.

Indeed, the ceremony also told a story of British exceptionalism. The choice to join the Common Market in the 1970s did not quite make the cut for the moments depicted in the opening ceremony. Our four-and-a-half decades as reluctant members of the European club are an important part of our recent political history, deciding the fate of more than one Prime Minister, but harder to place in the grand sweep of our national story across the centuries.

Peter Hitchens, taking part in a *Newsnight* discussion with me this week, was having none of this. Elevating the position of professional curmudgeon almost to that of being a national treasure, he could not see how a ceremony that was positive about the 1960s, and included rap music, had anything to say to those with a more traditional sense of identity.

Hitchens felt conscripted into a sense of "compulsory joy", complaining of feeling pressured to say that he liked the ceremony – which is, naturally, a matter of personal taste and opinion. But that anti-ceremony view was not very widely shared. The ceremony's inclusion of Jerusalem, Nimrod and Abide with Me, as well as Dizzee Rascal, may explain why its story of British pride did prove broadly popular with Britons of both a conservative and a liberal disposition. People did feel that the ceremony represented their sense of Britishness, by a margin of 65% to 67% in attitudes research conducted shortly after the games, with similar margins of six-to-one agreeing that it was entertaining and that it represented a positive balance between traditional and modern.

Perhaps that was even more striking in the Scottish referendum of 2014, a vote about whether to break up Britain itself. Danny Boyle was much more aware, in 2012, than the London Olympic organisers would have been in 1948 or 1908 that British identity had become a more complex thing. His ceremony opened with songs from the four nations and images of them competing against each other on the rugby field.

The themes of the opening ceremony featured in the Scottish independence referendum too, even if Danny Boyle's Olympic poetry got lost in the dour sceptical prose of a Scottish pro-Union campaign that became rather more "No Thanks" than "Better Together". What was striking was how the pro-independence side staked its own claim to those shared and popular British institutions. There was reassurance about the monarchy and the BBC as well as an argument about keeping the pound. Indeed, the Yes campaign's final push placed just as much emphasis on the NHS as the opening ceremony had. "We must leave Britain to keep Danny Boyle's flame alive," was the counter-intuitive message of a Yes campaign which argued that Scottish independence was now necessary to preserve the jewel in the crown of the post-war British welfare settlement.

Most pro-independence Scots who wish their team was carrying their own flag into the Rio stadium will cheer for Andy Murray during these Olympics, just as their political opponents would have done had the referendum result been different. That doesn't make sport more important than politics – but the value of national identity is that it can unite those who are deeply divided over even the most foundational issues.

We are still the country we were during that Olympic summer – a country that can be anxious and confident, with a strong sense of our history and identity, and with different views about what that should mean for the choices we make today. Perhaps it is our awareness that we can be a fragmented and fractured society – by class, by place and by politics – that gives us an appetite for the moments that bring us together.

5 August 2016

⇨ The above information is reprinted with kind permission from British Future. Please visit www.britishfuture.org for further information.

Cornwall and Yorkshire show regional identities run deep in England, too

An article from **The Conversation.** THE CONVERSATION

By Pete Woodcock, Head of the Division of Criminology, Politics and Sociology, University of Huddersfield

We are living in an increasingly decentralised UK. Devolution to Scotland, Wales and Northern Ireland – along with the Scottish independence referendum and a rise in nationalistic sentiment – have posed obvious opposition to the idea of the UK as a nation state.

Yet recent research and articles suggest that there are further challenges looming – particularly within England. As Matthew Johnson puts it, there is "a feeling that British politicians define English interests as those of London", and that "those in the northeast, northwest, and southwest have their own ideas about identity".

These ideas differ from the dominant London-centric concept of Englishness. Issues of English devolution are currently framed for the most part in economic terms, especially by mainstream parties – as epitomised by Osborne's attempt to manufacture a Northern Powerhouse. But my research suggests that there is more to Englishness – and that territorial identities may play a key role.

Cornwall: a Celtic nation

There has been a growing sense of politicisation among English regional identities in recent years, and nowhere more so than in Cornwall and Yorkshire. The Cornish have always had a distinct sense of cultural identity, which is different to Englishness. They would reject the description of Cornishness as a sub-national English identity. Instead, the Cornish people would argue that they identify as a nation on the same grounds as other members of the Celtic League – an organisation that campaigns for the political rights of Celtic nations such as Scotland, Ireland, Wales, Mann and Brittany.

This stance has had a political edge since the 1970s when Mebyon Kernow (MK) – previously a pressure group aimed at promoting Cornish culture, pursuits and history – started fielding candidates in elections. And yet, such politicisation of Cornishness is not confined only to regionalist parties such as MK (whose electoral results have been, all in all, rather marginal).

The Liberal Democrats – which used to consider Cornwall a stronghold – played a part in this as well. Through their position in the Coalition Government, the Lib Dems had an instrumental role in the process that led to Cornwall receiving special minority status in 2014. In the past, the Lib Dems strategically exploited Cornish identity for electoral ends, so as to maintain a support base in the area. More recently, the party pledged to form a Cornish Assembly if returned to government, a prospect which was shattered by the outcome of the election which saw the Lib Dems devastated across the country, and the Conservatives take all the parliamentary seats in Cornwall.

Yorkshire (first?)

Yorkshire is also often defined as having a distinct regional identity. There are around ten times as many people living in Yorkshire as in Cornwall, and the region's population is roughly the same as Scotland's. The Yorkshire identity seems to have solidified even further in the wake of the Scottish independence referendum, and the resulting plans to devolve more powers to Scotland.

Scotland now has greater influence both "at home" and at Westminster, and this has prompted claims that Yorkshire should also have a form of devolved government, comparable to that of Scotland.

Indeed, this is the platform of Yorkshire First – a regionalist political party created in 2014, which contested 14 seats in the general election. Although Yorkshire First had little electoral success this time around, it is a young political party finding its feet in national politics, and would have been using this election as testing ground for future campaigns.

The importance of identity

In the build up to the 2014 Scottish referendum, I conducted an online survey on identity and attitudes to devolution of power in both Cornwall and Yorkshire. I used what's called the "Moreno question", which allows for some subtlety in the way respondents can define their identity. It recognises that people do not necessarily define themselves in binary terms.

The survey asked if people regarded their identity as best described as:

⇨ Only Cornish/Yorkshire not English

⇨ More Cornish/Yorkshire not English

⇨ Equally Cornish/Yorkshire as English

⇨ More English than Cornish/Yorkshire

⇨ Only English not Cornish/Yorkshire.

The first finding that emerged was that, perhaps unsurprisingly, Cornish people often linked their identity to their Celtic heritage, and to a separateness from Englishness.

More than half of the respondents rejected any notion of Englishness in their identity, a quarter prioritised Cornishness over Englishness. Few claimed that English was their primary identity. So for a lot of Cornish people, being Cornish is not compatible with being English, and the former excludes the latter.

In Yorkshire, however, one sees a greater layering of identity. Fewer people – just under 15% of respondents – defined their identity as solely Yorkshire. The majority of people regard themselves as more Yorkshire than English, or equally Yorkshire as English. This means that there is no contradiction between Yorkshireness and Englishness – although being from Yorkshire is important to one's identity. This is not a nationalist claim like the one made by the Cornish, but it nonetheless illustrates that people regard Yorkshire as being important to their identity.

So evidence from both Yorkshire and Cornwall shows that regional and national dimensions are important to people's identity. However, people from the two areas may layer their identities in different manners. "Cornishness" appears to be more organic and homogenous, in that it is an identity with significant history, which is seen as a separate entity, distinct from Englishness. In contrast, "Yorkshireness" is still generally conflated with Englishness. But this does not make one identity less strong or less relevant than the other.

Devo deals?

Now, one might assume that demands for devolution of power would be greater in areas that have a strong sense of national identity than in areas with more regional identities. For our purposes, this would mean that the Cornish would want devolution of power more than those from Yorkshire. Yet this study shows that this is not the case.

[Research has shown]* very similar demands for the devolution of power in both Cornwall and Yorkshire, despite the differences in the way these identities are constructed. Although regional identities (such as Yorkshireness) are less bound to the concept of self-determination than national ones, this does not mean that they cannot be linked to political goals.

All of this goes to suggest that there is a connection between regional and national identities, and devolution claims within England. And that we should be wary of thinking about regional politics purely in economic terms.

*See original article for graph.

12 May 2015

⇨ The above information is reprinted with kind permission from *The Conversation*. Please visit www.theconversation.com for further information.

Multiculturalism can foster a new kind of Englishness

THE CONVERSATION

An article from **The Conversation.**

By Tariq Modood, Professor of Sociology, Politics and Public Policy and Founding Director of the Centre for the Study of Ethnicity and Citizenship, University of Bristol

To many, multiculturalism as a political idea in Britain suffered a body blow in 2001. In the shock of 9/11 terrorism and after race riots in some northern English towns, many forecast that its days were numbered. If these blows were not fatal, multiculturalism was then surely believed to have been killed off by the 7/7 attacks in London in 2005 and the terrorism and hawkish response to it that followed. But this is far too simplistic.

And today, a multicultural identity among some ethnic minorities could help to create more of a sense of 'British identity' among the English.

Multiculturalism in Britain grew out of an initial commitment to racial equality in the 1960s and 1970s into one of positive self-definition for minorities. One of the most significant pivots in this transition was *The Satanic Verses* affair of 1988–89, following the fatwa against its author Salman Rushdie, which mobilised Muslim identity in a way that ultimately grew to overshadow much other multiculturalist and anti-racist politics.

It is significant that multiculturalism in Britain has long had this bottom-up character, unlike say Canada and Australia, where the federal government has been the key initiator.

The Labour legacy

Nevertheless, anti-racism and multiculturalism in Britain still required governmental support and commitment. The first New Labour term between 1997 and 2001 has probably been the most multiculturalist national government in Britain – or indeed Europe.

Its initiatives included the funding of Muslim and other faith schools, the MacPherson Inquiry into institutional racism in the London Metropolitan Police and the Race Relations (Amendment) Act 2000, which strengthened previous equality legislation. This agenda continued to some extent in the second and third New Labour Governments, primarily with the extension of religious equality in law.

Yet, after 2001, and especially after the 2005 London bombings, there were significant departures from the earlier multiculturalism. But it is inaccurate to understand those developments as the end of multiculturalism. They mark its 'rebalancing' in order to give due emphasis to what we have in common as well as respect for difference.

At a local level, this consisted of programmes of community cohesion. This was premised on the idea of plural communities but was designed to cultivate interaction and co-operation, both at the micro level of people's lives and at the level of towns, cities and local government.

At a macro level, it consisted of emphasising national citizenship. Not in an anti-multiculturalist way as in France – where difference is regarded as unrepublican – but as a way of bringing the plurality into a better relationship with its parts. Definitions of Britishness offered under new Labour, for example, in the 2003 Crick report, emphasised that modern Britain was a multi-national, multicultural society, that there were many ways of being British and these were changing. As ethnic minorities became more woven into the life of the country they were redefining what it meant to be British.

The idea that an emphasis on citizenship or Britishness was a substitute for multiculturalism is quite misleading. The 2000 report of the Commission on the Future of Multi-Ethnic Britain – known as the Parekh Report, after its chair the Labour peer, Bhikhu Parekh – made national identity and "re-telling the national story", central to its understanding of equality, diversity and cohesion. It was the first public document to advocate the idea of citizenship ceremonies, arguing that citizenship and especially the acquisition of citizenship through naturalisation was – in contrast to countries like the US and Canada – undervalued in Britain.

Questions of Englishness

Yet over the last couple of decades a new set of challenges have become apparent, initially in Scotland but increasingly throughout the UK. In none of the nations of the union does the majority of the population consider themselves British, without also considering themselves English, Welsh, Scottish or Northern Irish first.

The 2011 census is not a detailed study of identity but it is striking that 70% of the people of England ticked the 'English' box and the vast majority of them did not also tick the 'British' box, even though they were invited to tick more than one. This was much more the case with white people than non-whites, who were more likely to be "British" only or combined with English. Multiculturalism, then, may actually have succeeded in fostering a British national identity among the ethnic minorities.

Multiculturalism in this case, then, offers not only the plea that English national consciousness should be developed in a context of a broad, differentiated British identity. But also, ethnic minorities can be seen as an important bridging group between those who think of themselves as only English, and those who consider themselves English and British.

Paradoxically, a supposedly out-of-date political multiculturalism becomes a source of how to think about not just integration of minorities but about how to conceive of our plural nationality and of how to give expression to dual identities such as English-British. It is no small irony that minority groups who are all too often seen as harbingers of fragmentation could prove to be exemplars of the union.

The minimum I would wish to urge upon a centre-left that is taking English consciousness seriously is that it should not be simply nostalgic and should avoid ethnic nationalism, such as talk of Anglo-Saxonism. More positively, multiculturalism, with its central focus on equal citizenship and diverse identities and on the renewing and reforging of nationality to make it inclusive of contemporary diversity, can help strengthen an appreciation of the emotional charge of belonging together.

10 June 2016

Will you become a citizen of Asgardia, the first nation state in space?

Aiming to open up access to space technology, protect Earth from cosmic threats and foster peace, proposals for a new space nation have been unveiled.

By Nicola Davis

Proposals for the "first nation state in space" have been unveiled by a team of scientists and legal experts, who say the move will foster peace, open up access to space technologies and offer protection for citizens of planet Earth.

Dubbed "Asgardia" after one of the mythical worlds inhabited by the Norse gods, the team say the "new nation" will eventually become a member of the United Nations, with its own flag and anthem devised by members of the public through a series of competitions.

According to the project website, Asgardia "will offer an independent platform free from the constraint of a land-based country's laws. It will become a place in orbit which is truly 'no man's land'".

Initially, it would seem, this new nation will consist of a single satellite, scheduled to be launched next year, with its citizens residing firmly on terra firma.

Speaking to *The Guardian* through an interpreter, the project lead Igor Ashurbeyli, said: "Physically the citizens of that nation state will be on Earth; they will be living in different countries on Earth, so they will be a citizen of their own country and at the same time they will be citizens of Asgardia."

"When the number of those applications goes above 100,000 we can officially apply to the UN for the status of state," he added.

According to the project website: "Any human living on Earth can become a citizen of Asgardia," with the site featuring a simple registration form. At the time of writing more than 1,000 individuals had already signed up.

When asked why people should register to become citizens of Asgardia, Ashurbeyli said: "I do believe that as soon as this country becomes a part of the UN family, citizenship of that country will be really quite prestigious."

A Russian businessman and nanoscientist who also founded the Vienna-based Aerospace International Research Center and is currently chairman of UNESCO's Science of Space committee, Ashurbeyli says the project aims to open up a conversation about regulations surrounding space activity.

At present, the Outer Space Treaty that underpins international space law states that responsibility and liability for objects sent into space lies with the nation that launched them.

But the project team claim that Asgardia will set a new precedent, shifting responsibility to the new "space nation" itself.

"The existing state agencies represent interests of their own countries and there are not so many countries in the world that have those space agencies," said Ashurbeyli.

"The ultimate aim is to create a legal platform to ensure protection of planet Earth and to provide access to space technologies for those who do not have that access at the moment."

Christopher Newman, an expert in space law at the UK's University of Sunderland, said the project reflects the fact that the geopolitical landscape of space activity has changed since the Outer Space Treaty was drawn up in the 1960s.

But, he added, it was not clear how Asgardia would fit into current international regulations, with the project facing significant hurdles, from getting UN recognition for Asgardia, to issues around liability.

"It is an exciting development in many ways because it will be interesting to see how this goes," said Newman. "But there are formidable obstacles in international space law for them to overcome. What they are actually advocating is a complete re-visitation of the current space law framework."

Ashurbeyli says the hope is that Asgardia will eventually become an official "launch state". But, he admits,

at least in the short term, cooperation from other countries will be required.

While the project's proposals remain vague, the vision for Asgardia is lofty. The team say that one of their early plans is to create "a state-of-the-art protective shield for all humankind from cosmic, manmade and natural threats to life on Earth." Such threats, they say, include the dangers posed by space junk, and even asteroids. But, at present, details remain hazy about what form such a shield could take.

And while the project does not currently include plans to set up an Asgardian settlement in space, Ashurbeyli believes life beyond Earth will be vital to the future of humankind. "We are laying the foundations to make that possible in the distant future," he said.

12 October 2016

⇨ The above information is reprinted with kind permission from *The Guardian*. Please visit www.theguardian.com for further information.

How the *Great British Bake Off* became the great British identity battle

An article from **The Conversation.**

THE CONVERSATION

By Clara Sandelind, Lecturer, University of Huddersfield

Of course Nadiya Hussain won the *Great British Bake Off* because she is a Muslim. For those unfamiliar with Islam, Victorian baking skills are a key element to this faith. Naturally she had an advantage.

Yes, bizarre as it may appear for those who have been following the show and marvelling at the precise judgement of Paul Hollywood and Mary Berry, accusations are being thrown at the programme for choosing its winner on the basis of political correctness rather than merit.

None of us knows if Nadiya was the best baker. After all, only a few lucky people of the BBC crew have actually tasted the bakes. She may have fashioned a peacock entirely from chocolate and produced a perfect trio of wedding cakes while her opponent forgot to actually add sugar to his final bake, but some have nevertheless suggested that the BBC wanted a Muslim to win; that the broadcaster has a hidden politically correct agenda.

In a column in *The Sun*, Ally Ross dubbed the show "full-scale ideological warfare". He wrote:

"Turn up without a box tick to your name, some viewers reckon, and you can bake an exact replica of the Taj Mahal using shortbread fingers and meringue nests and it still won't be enough to win this most PC of BBC shows."

Others have, on the contrary, celebrated the variety of contestants battling it out over cakes and breads the past few months. The multicultural blend of bakers has been seen as the epitome of Britishness.

There are two competing understandings of Britishness at stake in this debate. One views the British identity as having been hijacked by a politically correct elite, which has forced multiculturalism upon an eroding Christian or secular British culture. Another sees British identity as a celebration of a kind of difference that finds no difficulty in uniting around shared values, such as the virtue of a delightfully crisp pastry.

In its encapsulation of so-called banal nationalism – the everyday things that go to make up national identity – the *Great British Bake Off* has become the battlefield of national identity.

This battle includes a regrettable fixation with identity that characterises much of British politics more generally. Who you are is more important than what you do. Your class background matters if you are on the left; your gender matters for your views on feminism and your religious background matters for your views on terrorism. Have the wrong background combined with the wrong opinions and you will be betraying the working-class, abandoning women or simply be incomprehensible. We attach so much content to a specific identity that when someone deviates we cannot understand them.

The fact that we are having this debate at all is evidence of just how much is attached to a specific identity. Nadiya is also a mother of three and a student. Why are those identities not as important as her Muslim identity? Both on the left and the right, cultural and religious identity in particular has been elevated to a level at which it promises to explain everything about someone.

The battle of national identity is defined by the sentiment that a new kind of Britishness is being imposed from above by a corrupt elite. The BBC, as part of 'the establishment', is duping the population into accepting a multicultural Britishness that no one has chosen.

Yet national identity is constantly evolving. Those longing for a time of 'undiluted' Britishness are longing for an illusion. It is not uncommon for older generations to resent the culture of the new one, but culture is always changing. Immigration is one contributing factor to this change, but it is hardly the only one. Just think of the impact that smartphones have had on the way of life in modern Britain.

Discussions of who we are, on Britishness, are inevitable. The *Great British Bake Off* has a seemingly enormous unifying effect, precisely because of its expression of an inclusive Britishness. So identity is not redundant and it may even be necessary.

Yet the fixation of particular kinds of identities is debilitating for Britain as a society. Focus on identity and you may miss a good argument from someone. Focus on someone being a Muslim and you may miss a pretty tasty looking chocolate peacock.

8 October 2015

⇨ The above information is reprinted with kind permission from *The Conversation*. Please visit www.theconversation.com for further information.

Why it's time for an Office for Citizenship and Integration in London

On the anniversary of Britain's first citizenship ceremony, writes Steve Ballinger, a new report says that Britain has "forgotten" the value of citizenship and the importance of proactively promoting better integration – and calls on London to lead the way.

London is a city of immigration and that brings pressures on people living here, as well as economic and cultural benefits that have helped make our city one of the greatest in the world. Making integration work – for people already here and for new arrivals too – is one of the keys to London's continuing success. So we need a London that we can all share. We need to promote more contact and understanding between Londoners from different backgrounds. And we need to build a sense of citizenship that reaches and matters to Londoners born and raised in Britain as much as to this country's newest arrivals.

That's why we're calling on all London mayoral candidates to back a new proposal for an Office for Citizenship and Integration at the GLA.

A new report setting out the proposals, from British Future in partnership with London Citizens, the largest and most diverse civic partnership in the capital, and backed by voices across party politics, sets out why London needs to do more to promote integration and citizenship, and some of the key priorities that the new office could pursue. These include:

⇨ Ensuring that more people speak English so they can fully be part of British life.

⇨ Promoting greater involvement in civic life and contact between people from different backgrounds, including through volunteering drives and encouraging all young Londoners to register and use their first vote, as a step towards understanding of the value of common citizenship.

⇨ Encouraging more migrants living in London to take British citizenship, with a target of increasing by 100,000 the rate of citizenship registrations over the four-year mayoral term.

The new proposals are backed by: Trevor Phillips OBE; David Lammy MP; Steve Norris, former Conservative London mayoral candidate; Mark Rimmer, Head of Registration and Nationality for the London Borough of Brent; Bharat Mehta, Chief Executive, Trust for London; Sonny Leong, Trustee, Mulan Foundation Network; Bite the Ballot; Moira Sinclair, Director, Paul Hamlyn Foundation; and Sara Llewellin, Chief Executive, Barrow Cadbury Trust.

Steve Norris, former Conservative Mayoral candidate, said:

"Integration is a vital way to ensure that people who come to our great city make their fullest contribution to it – so that London benefits economically and socially, and we handle the pressures of immigration in a way that is fair to everybody.

"So I welcome this practical proposal about how the next Mayor could get the foundations of integration right – to make sure everybody shares a common language and can talk to their neighbours, and to do more to celebrate the pride which new citizens have in becoming British.

"It is an idea that should appeal across the political parties. London Conservatives are increasingly confident about our ability to appeal to Londoners across every colour and creed, and I hope Zac Goldsmith and his campaign will see the proposal as an attractive way for the next Mayor to make a positive contribution to bringing our diverse city together".

Tottenham MP David Lammy commented:

"I fully support the establishment of the GLA's Office for Citizenship and Integration, which is a vital development in turning rhetoric on the benefits of immigration into action that will benefit both immigrants and the city of London alike. As a country we don't yet 'do'

integration well enough and too many new arrivals consequently go on to live parallel lives in isolation, unable to make the most of the opportunities to thrive provided by our economy, culture and social fabric.

"We need to do much more and commit to a real concerted effort to enable new arrivals to fully integrate into our communities. The Office for Citizenship and Integration will be a valuable step forward in boosting integration by harnessing best practice and ensuring a joined-up approach across our city, which in turn can set the standard for improving how we encourage and promote integration across the country."

To launch the proposal, Citizens UK are inviting a group of young Londoners to witness a citizenship ceremony in Brent, followed by a workshop to explore what citizenship means to them and what they feel a new Deputy Mayor could do to promote citizenship and integration. Keren Fadega, Blood, Sweat and Tears Leader for Citizens UK said:

"We need one London that's fair for all of us – whether you've just arrived here or lived here all your life. And it's important that we keep on getting to know people from different backgrounds, learning from each other and being proud of our diversity. The politicians we elect to run London need to take responsibility for making that work, for everyone."

This is something for all Londoners, of all backgrounds. Integration should not be seen as a challenge only for migrants and minority groups. The new Deputy Mayor should champion a vision, relevant to London and well beyond it, of integration as a shared challenge for us all

This agenda can be pursued effectively at limited cost, with existing GLA resources supplemented by philanthropic partners in the city and charitable foundations. A new London citizenship fund could be created pulling private and public monies together, aiming to agree pledges that will total £1 million in private donations, with the expectation that they would be matched by the Mayor.

London is already an integration success story compared to most other world capitals. But with a dynamic individual driving forward a proactive plan, London could do so much more, becoming a beacon for more successful integration across the whole of Britain and helping to develop a stronger, shared sense of what integration means and how it can work in practice.

Mark Rimmer OBE, Head of Registration and Nationality for Brent and Barnet Councils – and the registrar who presided over the first citizenship ceremony on 26 February 2004 – said:

"I have been involved in conducting citizenship ceremonies since the very first one 12 years ago. I have seen first hand the passion, pride and emotion that participation in ceremonies generates and I feel privileged to have been a part of these life-defining events.

"The introduction of a welcoming event to celebrate the acquisition of British citizenship was a great step forward but I do feel that we now lack a political champion to take the initiative to the next stage. It is important that our new citizens feel welcomed and valued by our politicians – to encourage belonging and integration and to celebrate those who wish to join us as part of the British family."

Trevor Phillips OBE, former Chair of the Equalities and Human Rights Commission, said:

"London is a beacon of integration in the modern world – but in a world that is changing as quickly as ours, effective integration won't happen by accident. It has to be an active process – promoted, negotiated and supported in workplaces, schools and neighbourhoods. That's why an office isn't just another bureaucratic invention – it's a vital part of the city's economic and social future."

Bharat Mehta, Chief Executive of Trust for London, said:

"London could be the place that all aspirational cities across the world want to emulate. Our global city attracts people from all over the world, who together, bring much to its economy and culture. It is important that we promote London's strengths, including its amazing diversity. A dedicated Office for Citizenship and Integration would provide a focal point for these efforts, ensuring that Londoners benefit from the proactive inclusion of people who choose to make the capital their home and the United Kingdom their country."

Michael Sani, Chief Executive of Bite the Ballot, said:

"BTB would welcome all mayoral candidates and the next mayor to put a greater emphasis on civic participation for all Londoners. Greater civic engagement and an emphasis on active citizenship will ensure community cohesion and empowerment across London."

25 February 2016

⇨ The above information is reprinted with kind permission from British Future. Please visit www.britishfuture.org for further information.

Are you a global citizen? New poll suggests global trumps national identity

By Jenny Soffel

More and more people around the world identify themselves as global citizens rather than citizens of their country, according to a BBC World Service poll conducted by GlobeScan.

The big increase of this sentiment is being driven largely by emerging economies, such as Nigeria (73% feel they are global citizens), China (71%), Peru (70%) and India (67%).

"73% of Nigerians feel they are global citizens"

Over 20,000 people worldwide in 18 countries took part in the poll, and it's the first time in 15 years of tracking that more than half of the respondents saw themselves as global citizens rather than national citizens.

Conversely, the poll indicates a growing divide between industrialised countries and developing economies. Before the financial crisis in 2008, the concept of global citizenship was equally supported in both country groupings. But since 2009, the trend has followed a downwards trajectory, with Germany hitting the all-time low with only 30% of respondents identifying themselves as global.

"The poll indicates a growing divide between industrialised countries and developing economies"

Among richer nations, 59% of those asked in Spain considered themselves to be more global than national, followed by Greece (47%), the UK (47%), Germany (30%), and Russia (24%).

28 April 2016

⇨ The above information is reprinted with kind permission from the World Economic Forum. Please visit www.weforum.org for further information.

What does it mean to be a citizen?

The question of what does it mean to be a citizen has no simple answer. On a purely definition-based description, what it means to be a citizen is that a person is a legally recognised inhabitant of the country they live in – in the UK, this means they pay taxes and are entitled to the help of the benefits and NHS systems. However, in practice, answering the question what does it mean to be a citizen is far from easy. As new rules and tests for people wanting British citizenship show, being a citizen is about far more than a legal status. It is about understanding and accepting – and being a part of the culture, rather than an observer from the outside.

Understanding

Cultures are complex things to get a handle on. Depending on how different one person's home culture is to another's, there may be huge gaps in understanding of each other's cultures. To truly be a citizen of a country, the person must fully understand its culture. This does not necessarily mean that person must blindly agree with the ways of doing things – but an understanding of how and why things happen is vital. In fact, the greater their understanding of a culture, the

more people – citizens – may want to question it. But in many ways, this is human nature at work. And, if a deeper understanding of the culture leads to a deeper dissatisfaction of the way things are done, then so be it. A right to protest and the act of protesting are all signs that a person is a citizen in the truest sense of the word – because they understand the culture and, although they disagree with things, they are involved enough to want to make a change, hopefully, for what they believe to be the greater good.

Accepting

But protestors who have the country's best interests at heart – and moreover those of the people who live in it – must take care not to damage the culture or the country. And in that way, they must be accepting of the culture. For example, a person in the UK who was anti-monarchy may set up petitions and hold organised and peaceful protests calling for its abolition. This is their right, and one would hope that in line with their views, what they would like to see happen. However, a non-peaceful protest against the monarchy would not be a good citizen's way of doing things – as it does show an acceptance

of the culture, and, moreover could be harmful to the people who live there.

Being a part of a culture

To truly be able to answer the question of what does it mean to be a citizen, a person must become part of their culture and part of their community. This is why there is now an English language requirement for new citizens of the UK. Not speaking the language the other people in your community and culture speak is a major hindrance to becoming a true citizen – with regards to being part of the culture. Being part of the culture though goes much further than this. It is about integration with others, about bringing your views and experiences to the table and sharing them to make the whole culture richer from the experience of everyone in it. It can be about having a public service job, about volunteering and about giving back. It is about working together for the greater good.

And therein lies the eternal answer to what does it mean to be a citizen. Legally, a citizen is someone who has the required passport, a piece of paper. But truly, a citizen is someone who shares with their communities and who gives back what they take out. Make no mistake, there are plenty of people in the UK who were born here but could not be said to be true citizens – it is about an emotional state and mindset just as much as a geographical and legal term.

13 November 2014

⇨ The above information is reprinted with kind permission from Responsible Citizen. Please visit www.responsiblecitizen.co.uk for further information.

© Responsible Citizen 2017

Previous nationalities granted citizenship
The chart below shows the top five nationalities granted citizenship. (Total number of grants in 2015–118,053)

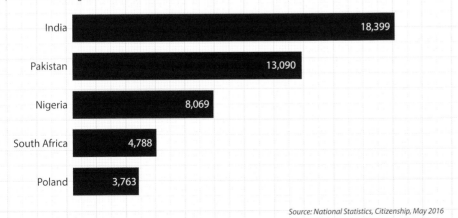

India 18,399
Pakistan 13,090
Nigeria 8,069
South Africa 4,788
Poland 3,763

Source: National Statistics, Citizenship, May 2016

Being a responsible citizen

Everyone has a duty to be a responsible citizen. But unfortunately, not everyone takes this responsibility seriously. There are plenty of people the world over who do not know what being a responsible citizen means and these are the people who destroy our communities. For being a responsible citizen results in a happy and harmonious community – if everyone else does the same.

Being a responsible citizen covers many areas – some of them legal obligations, some social and some moral. So of course, because not all of them are legal obligations, being a responsible citizen is not as easy as staying within the law. In fact, to be a truly responsible citizen, we sometimes must go out of our way to do things which help our society – give a little of our time and effort for the greater good.

Legal obligations

No one can be a responsible citizen without staying within the law. It is as simple as that. Criminals, by their very nature, are not behaving as responsible citizens. Laws exist to protect citizens, the communities they live in and their property. So to be a responsible citizen, we must respect these laws and abide by them. Harming others or others' property does not equate to being a good citizen.

Social obligations

Social obligations really form the bulk of being a responsible citizen and what this means. To be a responsible citizen, we should help our communities and those who live in them. So, being a responsible citizen can encompass things such as volunteering.

Volunteering, the third sector, is worth billions to our economy and even more to those who are helped by volunteering. But in the interests of being a responsible citizen, this could include smaller things too. So, volunteering for the Samaritans is a noble job to do and one which is certainly needed. But the elderly lady who lives alone may need someone to do her shopping and this demonstrates responsible citizenship just as much as volunteering in an organisation.

Other social obligations of being a good citizen can include things such as helping local businesses. This may means buying the meat for Sunday dinner from a local butcher rather than a supermarket, or using a small local bookstore rather than the Internet. Being a responsible citizen also means being involved in our communities. This may be demonstrated by being on the school parent teacher association or the village hall committee. It may be as simple as attending events organised by these people.

Moral obligations

Moral obligations of being a responsible citizen are harder to pin down because different people have different moral codes. But one place we can all start is in helping the environment.

The environmental problems society is facing are of our own making and we all have a moral obligation to do what we can to change this. So by living an environmentally friendly life as possible, we can help fulfil our moral obligations of being a responsible citizen. Taking recyclables to be recycled and using a compost bin are two easy ways and there are many more.

And they can be linked in with other obligations. For example, if you have a compost bin but no plants to use the compost on, you could give it to people who have plants but live alone, making them less likely to generate a huge amount of compost themselves.

Being a responsible citizen should not be a hard thing but it should be something which occasionally requires a little extra effort. This is because being a responsible citizen is, at its core, about being a less selfish person, and putting the needs of society before your own needs. It does not means you have to sacrifice all your free time to volunteer or help others, but it does means taking a little time to think about the impact of your actions on others.

26 October 2016

⇨ The above information is reprinted with kind permission from Responsible Citizen. Please visit www.responsiblecitizen.co.uk for further information.

Education can provide both the opportunities and capabilities to make active citizens of our young people

The general election once again showed the extent of yawning divide in terms of political participation between older and younger citizens. James Sloam and Ben Kisby reflect on the extent to which young people (dis)engage from politics. By analysing data from the European Social Survey (ESS), they conclude that educational institutions are a vital factor in influencing young people's levels of disengagement.

Much attention has been paid by academics and policy-makers in recent decades to declining levels of voter turnout and engagement with traditional political and social institutions in established democracies – from political parties to trade unions to religious organisations. These trends are particularly marked among young people. Nevertheless, a number of authors have, more positively, pointed to the proliferation of youth participation in a myriad of alternative forms of engagement. If we take a broad look at political participation – focussing on what young people are actually doing rather than what they are not doing – it is in fact possible to conclude that the Millennial Generation are at least as politically active as previous generations. In this sense, they continue to have a voice. However, these changes in political and civic engagement raise new questions about inequalities in participation and the nature of political socialisation.[1]

Young people have increasingly become 'standby citizens' who engage from time to time with political issues that hold meaning for their everyday lives.[2] In general, they are attracted to intermittent, non-institutionalised, issue-based, horizontal forms of engagement and repelled by the thought of long-term commitment through formal institutions with broader policy goals and entrenched hierarchies. As well as young people's repertoires of participation having changed, the political arenas in which they operate have also become more diverse, including, in particular, online social networks. The rise of the Internet and new social media has enabled a quickening of political participation that promotes real-time engagement in politics and non-hierarchical forms of mobilisation.

Whereas voting is generally considered to be a relatively socially equal political act (at least in Western Europe, this is much less so in the United States), the same, however, cannot be said for alternative forms of engagement, such as signing a petition, joining a boycott, participating in a demonstration, or utilising new social media. Recent research suggests that social inequalities are significantly increased in non-electoral forms of political engagement. Since young people are more likely to engage in these non-electoral forms of participation than older cohorts, our concern is with whether this translates into political participation that is less socially equal for young Europeans, and we are interested in what role education might play in mitigating these inequalities. The literature on civic and citizenship education suggests that personal efficacy plays a key role in actualising young people's politics, whereby the political literacy, democratic skills and self-confidence of young citizens are of fundamental importance.[3]

Drawing on the most recent data available from ESS, which is undertaken every two years, we have found that being in education significantly boosts young people's civic and political participation helping neutralise the differences between high-income and low-income groups with regard to such participation.

Data shows that:

⇨ Young people, here 18- to 21-year-olds, are less engaged in traditional, electoral politics (especially voting) than the general population, but as engaged in other forms of participation. Being in education clearly matters a great deal because those in education are more active than the general population in all forms of participation except voting and contact (although the gap here is not that large) and have higher levels of social and political trust.

⇨ 18- to 21-year-olds in higher education have similar levels of engagement in electoral politics as the mean figure for all ages, but are much more likely to engage in all other forms of participation than the general population. They also have higher levels of social and political trust than the general population and are much more likely to sign petitions, participate in demonstrations and join boycotts than 18-21 year olds not in higher education.

⇨ Being in education boosts participation for 18–21s in almost all political acts, especially for those from low income backgrounds, who actually outperform those from high income backgrounds in education for working for an organisation or association, signing a petition, going on a demonstration, or participating in a boycott. It also shows that 18- to 21-year-olds in education from low income backgrounds outperform those from high income backgrounds who are not in education on these measures, as well as being significantly more likely to vote.

1 Sloam, J. (2014) *New Voice, Less Equal: The Civic and Political Engagement of Young People in the United States and Europe*, Comparative Political Studies, 47(5): 663-688.

2 Amnå, E. and Ekman, J. (2014) *Standby citizens: diverse faces of political passivity*, European Political Science Review, 6(2): 261-281.

3 Kisby, B. (2012) *The Labour party and citizenship education: policy networks and the introduction of citizenship lessons in schools*, (Manchester: Manchester University Press).

The ESS data shows that the most active in most forms of civic and political participation are those with a high education (see Table 1). Interestingly, it would seem that being in education neutralises the differences between high-income and low-income groups with regards to levels of civic and political participation. The key question is why? In our view, this is likely to be due to the political socialisation effect of educational establishments, which provide students with social networks and a culture of participation, underpinned by a relatively democratic ethos. It is not possible to test this claim with the ESS data, but it is consistent with the findings of the Citizenship Education Longitudinal Study, which has been surveying the civic learning, behaviour, and attitudes of young people in England since 2001[4].

We draw two main conclusions from our analysis of the ESS data. First, educational institutions play a vital role in scaffolding the transition of young people into adulthood, for example, by providing them with opportunities to engage in forms of civic and political activity. And second, educational establishments play a key role as social levellers, as they are particularly effective in providing a platform for civic and political engagement for young people from deprived backgrounds. In our view, this places added emphasis on the role of educational organisations in nurturing such engagement.

19 May 2015

⇨ The above information is reprinted with kind permission from The Crick Centre. Please visit www.crickcentre.org for further information.

© The Crick Centre 2017

4 Keating, A., Kerr, D., Benton, T., Mundy, E. and Lopes, J. (2010) *Citizenship Education in England 2001–2010: young people's practices and prospects for the future: the eighth and final report from the Citizenship Education Longitudinal Study*, (London: DfE); see also http://www.llakes.org/the-citizenship-education-longitudinal-study-cels/

Does volunteering make you happier?

Here at Join In, we often see the effect that volunteering has on people. We love hearing how rewarding our volunteers find it to help others, and make a difference in their communities. So we decided to look into the subject a little bit more with an independent online survey.

Carried out in April 2014 by Delta Value and Morar Research, we surveyed over 2,500 people from a controlled population of clubs and volunteers in the Join In database, as well as the general public.

What did we find?

Well, the research showed that, when compared to a group that had never volunteered in sport, those that had volunteered were less likely to feel unhappy or depressed. Interestingly, there was also a direct correlation between happiness and the longevity of volunteering – as those who had volunteered in sport for ten plus years gave the most positive responses. Here are some of the stats:

⇨ 88% of people agreed they had a lot to be proud of

⇨ 87% said their life has more meaning because of volunteering

⇨ People who volunteer in sport have a 10% higher self-esteem, emotional wellbeing and resilience than those who have never volunteered

⇨ Those who have never volunteered in sport are more likely to feel unhappy, sad or depressed

⇨ Sports volunteers are 15% less likely to worry, and less likely to feel anxious or cry a lot

⇨ They are 28% more likely to feel what they do has importance

These results back up what we hear throughout the year from the thousands of people involved in Join In. Here are just a few of the messages we've received from them about the positive impact of volunteering:

"I want as many people as possible to experience the sense of pride and honour I feel to be a part of something so special. As a volunteer at a grassroots club, you are an integral part of creating childhood memories, friendships and experiences that will stay with these kids for their whole life."

"I had panic attacks when I split up with my husband and couldn't travel on trains anymore. Being accepted as a Games Maker for London 2012 made me tackle that fear."

"Volunteering makes me feel lucky and privileged, proud and valued. I feel needed and like I make a difference by offering lots of brilliant kids a positive activity."

20 May 2014

⇨ The above information is reprinted with kind permission from Join in. Please visit www.joininuk.org for further information.

© Join in 2017

How can I get involved in campaigning?

Information on how you can join a campaign or start your own!

If you feel strongly about an issue (whether it's in school, your club or your area) and want to do something about it, there will probably already be a group dedicated to the issue that you could join. If there isn't see if any of your friends or family feel the same way. There may also be a local youth group or council in your area that you could join to raise the issue and people's awareness. If not, you could start your own group or Youth Council and try to get people interested.

There's other things you can do to raise awareness like: put up posters; ask around; hand out fliers; design your own website. It's all about getting people thinking.

There are people around to help – start with your local youth/community workers. Phone the local council to find out details about your nearest project/office.

Starting a petition

Gathering other people's support from your community is a good way to get weight behind your campaign.

Start a petition collecting signatures and addresses written next to your statement and your name, as the petitioner. This can be submitted at all levels of government, whether it's to your local council, Scottish Parliament, central government or European Parliament.

The contents of the petition could be a matter of public concern, e.g. pollution in a river, or of a more individual interest. The petition should be submitted to the relevant level of government with responsibility for that topic. It should not relate to any current court proceedings.

Each level of government has guidelines about what is acceptable and will advise on this. Don't underestimate this as a tool for change as it really can make a difference, as well as generally raising awareness.

Direct action

You may feel that you are acting more directly by marching or becoming involved in a protest, demonstration or sit-in. These forms of protest do get some profile in the media. However, the law says the protest or demonstration organiser must apply to the local council for permission to do this. Some organisations are exempt from this procedure – write to your council to find out if your group is on their list.

It is important to be able to protest in the right manner and make sure you are not breaking the law – e.g. trespassing, breach of the peace. You don't want your cause to be discredited because of your actions.

Use the media

Use the media to highlight your cause. This is a very useful and powerful tool in generating awareness and support for your cause if used wisely. You want to get the media on your side.

When writing to the press, address any letters to 'The Editor', give your name and address, and hopefully your letter will be printed. Go that step further and think seriously about persuasive press releases, set up contacts, and be nice so reporters come back to you again and again.

Use short snappy headlines emphasising the 'who, what, where, why, how' behind your project. Write to national newspapers, your local newspaper, your school magazine, the Young Scot magazine, or the Young Scot website.

Consider local radio too, as this form of media can reach many people instantly, and its power can be underestimated.

Using the Internet

With web pages within everyone's reach, an effective campaign can be carried out from your own sitting room via the Internet.

You can use a specially designed site to gauge public feeling, gather comments and survey visitors, or use your social networking sites (e.g Facebook or Twitter) to gather support. Then you need to pass on your findings to the relevant decision-makers. You could also broadcast live on the web, or contribute to radio stations.

⇨ The above information is reprinted with kind permission from Young Scot. Please visit young.scot for further information.

Thousands of young people doing their bit for society? Let's be more ambitious

We should expand the National Citizen Service to all 16- and 17-year-olds. It's those who are hardest to reach who would benefit from the sense of purpose it creates.

By Dan Jarvis

People often say to me that we should re-introduce national service: that some basic military discipline would imbue our young people with a sense of purpose and direction. But rather than going back to the 1950s, we should look for new ways to harness the ideals of service in a way that works for young people in Britain today.

Times have changed and so have the attitudes of today's youth. The *Generation Citizen* report from Demos found that teenagers are more engaged in social issues than any previous generation. Yet service is still important. For a young person, having the opportunity to serve – whether it be participating in the Duke of Edinburgh's award scheme, or scouts, or the National Citizen Service – can help lay vital foundations for adult life.

Ghandi said: "The best way to find yourself is to lose yourself in the service of others" – and there is a critical link between service and society: it is by helping others that we best show our solidarity and sense of shared humanity. Anyone who pays taxes does this to some extent, but it is a far less direct way of cementing the bonds between us.

The vast majority of people care about their local community – whether they are rich or poor, and regardless of age. Many seek to make a contribution through service. The Games Makers from the London 2012 Olympics and Paralympics are a standout example. Future First is another: it has recruited more than 100,000 state school alumni across the country to act as role models for the next generation in state education.

The National Citizen Service – a vision of the last Labour Government brought to life by the Coalition – is proving its worth as another, more widespread route for service. It is a scheme that gives young people the opportunity to take part in team-building exercises, learn new skills and participate in practical community volunteering in their area. It has seen year-on-year increases in the number of participants, with more than 55,000 young people last year. But I think we need to be more ambitious.

The most recent independent evaluation showed that NCS delivers as much as £3.98 of benefit for every £1 spent. Yet if 55,000 young people are participating in this great programme, that means there are hundreds of thousands who still are not. Those who are the hardest to reach are often the ones who would benefit most from the sense of purpose and community that service creates. They would find real value from the teamwork, social mixing and camaraderie. These are the young people whose potential risks being wasted, and for whom a programme like this could offer a chance to shape their future for the better.

So I think we should look to expand the National Citizen Service, so all young people aged 16 and 17 have the opportunity to take part. We should also look at how we best support other great programmes that allow young people to serve – schemes such as City Year, which recruits people aged 18–25 to volunteer full time as role models, mentors and tutors at schools in deprived areas over the course of an academic year.

Schemes like this are crucial not just because of the social value they add, but because they would help build on the NCS programme. Service should not just be a month-long programme, but a lifetime mission. It has the potential to help transform our society. The case for supporting it is all the stronger in a time where in many places it feels like the bonds of community are loosening. If as a society we embrace service, then we will find that serving others serves us all.

13 April 2016

⇨ The above information is reprinted with kind permission from *The Guardian*. Please visit www.theguardian.com for further information.

"The best way to find yourself is to lose yourself in the service of others."

Political disengagement in the UK: who is disengaged?

Young people

Attitudes

While 18- to 24-year-olds are more likely to report a low level of knowledge about politics, they do not necessarily hold more negative attitudes towards the political system overall.

Young people have a slightly more positive view of democracy's responsiveness to their interests than other age groups do (apart from the 60+ group), but are also more likely to report that they do not know how well the system addresses their interests.

Political activities

Research using social surveys suggests young people are more likely to think that getting involved is effective. This attitude does not translate into action: 18- to 24-year-olds are less likely to say they have participated in political activities, or would do so if they cared strongly about an issue.

Electoral registration

Evidence suggests that young people are less likely to be on the electoral register than older people, although some variation exists between younger age groups.

A 2014 Electoral Commission study identified some differences between young people based on their level of qualification.

In England and Wales, 78.5% of 18- to 34-year-olds educated to degree level (or equivalent) were estimated to be on the electoral register in April 2011, compared to only 63.3% of those with no qualifications.

The Electoral Commission notes that in part, lower levels of registration among young people are explained by the fact that young people move house more often, and mobility has a strong impact on registration.

Voting

Young people are also less likely to vote than older people. The IPPR's 2013 report, *Divided Democracy*, notes that differences in turnout between age groups have increased over time.

Councillors, candidates, MPs

The average age of councillors, MPs and party members is over 50 years.

Ethnic minorities

Attitudes

The Hansard Society's 2015 *Audit of Political Engagement* showed that ethnic minorities were more likely to be satisfied with the democratic system in the UK than white people, but less likely to report a fair amount of knowledge about politics.

The figures hide differences between ethnic groups. Academic research shows that Black Africans and Black Caribbeans are more likely to be interested in politics than other ethnic minorities and white people. Bangladeshis are most likely to be satisfied with democracy in Britain, while also being the least interested in politics.

Research also shows that a high proportion of first-generation migrants (born abroad) believe in the duty to vote. This rate decreases to 81% in second generation migrants (born in the UK to at least one parent born abroad).

Political activities

The Hansard Society's 2015 Audit found that ethnic minorities were less likely than the white population to engage in political activities, or to do so if they felt strongly about an issue.

Electoral registration

Ethnic minorities are less likely to be included on the electoral register than white British people. Academics found that non-registration was much higher among ethnic minorities: 25% of the first generation and 20% of second-generation ethnic minorities who were eligible to register to vote had not done so, compared to 10% of the white British population.

A table in the Audit shows evidence that there are significant differences in under-registration among ethnic groups. This phenomenon is partly explained because some groups believe (often wrongly) that they are not entitled to be registered.

Voting

Ethnic minorities were more likely to believe in the duty to vote but were less likely to actually vote. Survey data suggests 56% of people from an ethnic minority background voted in the 2015 general election, compared to 68% of white people.

Councillors, candidates, MPs

In England 4% came from an ethnic minority. In Wales it was 0.8% and in Scotland the percentage of non-white councillors was similar to that of its population at 3.4%. Following the 2015 election, 6.3% of all MPs have been categorised as from non-white backgrounds.

Housing and occupational background

Socio-economic factors have been associated with political disengagement. Research suggests that ethnic minorities are less likely to be middle class, but significant differences exist between ethnic minority groups.

Unskilled workers and the long-term unemployed

Most studies of political disengagement use the 'social grade' classification system that distinguishes between people on the basis of their occupation. The grades are defined in the Audit.

Attitudes

The Hansard Society Audit found 62% of people in the C2DE social grades felt that "our democratic system does not address the interests of myself and my family very well or at all", compared to 53% of those in the social grades ABC1.

The Audit also found that renters are more likely to consider democracy unresponsive to their interests (63%) than homeowners (54%).

Political activities

Evidence also suggests that people from social grades DE are least likely to have participated in political activities, or to do so if they feel strongly about an issue.

Electoral registration

People from the DE social grades were less likely to be included on the 2014 electoral registers than people from other grades. People's housing situation was found to have a significant effect, as shown in a table in the Audit. Private renters tend to move house more often and the Electoral Commission suggests mobility is an important driver of low levels of registration.

Voting

People in the DE social grades are least likely to vote: 57% were estimated to have voted at the 2015 general election, compared to 75% in the AB social grades; 69% of those in the C1 social grade; and 62% of those in the C2 social grade.

Councillors, candidates, MPs

There is little information available on the social background of councillors, candidates and MPs. However, the 2013 Census of Local Authority Councillors noted that 58.8% of councillors were educated to degree level (or equivalent), while 13% were educated to GCE A-level (or equivalent) and 11.2% to GSCE level (or equivalent). 5.2% of councillors had no qualifications.

Women

Attitudes

Polling evidence suggests women are less likely to be satisfied with the political system than men. When asked "how well do you think democracy in Britain as a whole addresses the interests of people like you", men and women gave similar answers.

However, men were more likely than women to answer "not well at all" (19% of men, 12% of women), while women were more likely to answer "don't know" (6% of men, 13% of women).

Political activities

The Hansard Society's Audit of Political Engagement shows that women were also less likely than men to have engaged in political activities, and to say they would do so if they felt strongly about an issue.

Electoral registration

The Electoral Commission reported that women were slightly more likely to be on the February/March 2014 electoral registers than men (85.8% of women, 83.6% of men). In April 2011 this was 87% of women compared to 85.1% of men.

Voting

Surveys suggest men were slightly more likely to vote than women (but only by one to three percentage points) in the past four elections.

Councillors, candidates, MPs

In 2013, 32% of local authority councillors in England were women. In the North East (41%), in Scotland (24%), in Wales (26%) and Northern Ireland (23%).

191 women MPs were elected at the 2015 General Election, 29% of all MPs. Just over 35% of members in the Scottish Parliament are women, compared to two-fifths of members of National Assembly for Wales. Following the 2014 European Parliament elections, women comprised just over two-fifths of UK MEPs.

People with disabilities

Political activities

The Equality and Human Rights Commission found that in 2013/2014, there was no significant difference between the proportions of people with (31.7%) and without (29.7%) disabilities who had engaged in one or more of four political activities in the last 12 months.

Electoral registration

People with physical disabilities were more likely to be on the electoral register than any other group. The Electoral Commission suggests this might be because they are less likely to move home, and mobility is an important driver of low levels of registration.

A small-scale study of patients in psychiatric wards in Westminster found that only 43% of patients had registered to vote for the 2010 General Election, compared to 97% of the local eligible population. Of those registered to vote, only 33% had voted.

Voting

The charity Mencap claims that only one-third of people with learning disabilities in the UK vote. While no other data is available on turnout among people with disabilities in the UK, a 2002 study of voting among disabled people in the US showed that 52.6% of respondents with disabilities reported they had voted in the 1998 election, compared to 59.4% of respondents without disabilities.

Councillors, candidates, MPs

The 2013 Census of Local Authority Councillors reported that 13.2% of councillors had "a long-term health problem or disability". The Disability News Service reported in 2015 that there were two MPs who self-reported as having a disability.

Overseas voters

The Government does not keep track of citizens living abroad, so no information is available on their attitudes and levels of participation in political activities. It is difficult to calculate the total number of people who would be eligible to register as overseas voters.

The Political and Constitutional Reform Committee in its 2014 report on Voter engagement in the UK estimated that less than 1% of British citizens living abroad were registered to vote.

26 February 2016

⇨ The above information is reprinted with kind permission from the House of Commons Library. Please visit researchbriefings.parliament.uk for further information.

© House of Commons Library 2017

Child labour: at what age is it OK to get children engaged in politics?

It is not until the age of 15 that a majority of people think it is acceptable to have started encouraging a child to take an interest in politics.

By Matthew Smith

Last week a new Momentum-related group called Momentum Kids was launched. The group seeks to increase "children's involvement in Momentum and the labour movement by promoting political activity that is fun, engaging and child-friendly", whilst also providing childcare for parents and carers.

Momentum Kids will engage with children as young as three years old – activities publicised include imagining the party your favourite toy might lead and creating placards for a mock protest. But is it OK to encourage such young children to engage with politics? At what age does the public think it's OK for someone to start encouraging a child to get into politics?

New YouGov research finds that it is not until the age of 15 that a majority of people think it is OK to have started encouraging a child to take an interest in politics. There is a left/right split, however, with voters for left-wing parties more likely to think it is OK to politically encourage children at younger ages.

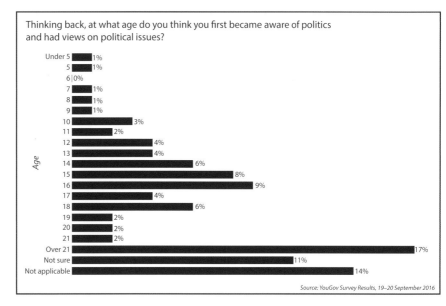

Thinking back, at what age do you think you first became aware of politics and had views on political issues?

Age	%
Under 5	1%
5	1%
6	0%
7	1%
8	1%
9	1%
10	3%
11	2%
12	4%
13	4%
14	6%
15	8%
16	9%
17	4%
18	6%
19	2%
20	2%
21	2%
Over 21	17%
Not sure	11%
Not applicable	14%

Source: YouGov Survey Results, 19–20 September 2016

The age by which the majority of Lib Dem voters think it is OK to have started politically encouraging children is 13, and it is 14 for Labour voters. For Conservative voters, that age is 15, and it is 16 for UKIP voters.

Left-wing voters are especially more keen on getting children engaged at younger ages. Nearly a quarter of Labour (24%) and Lib Dem (23%) voters think it is appropriate to have started politically encouraging a child by the age of ten (compared to 10% of Conservatives and 8% of Ukippers).

Far fewer voters support getting children engaged at very young ages. Momentum Kids itself will look after children as young as three years old, but just 3% of Labour voters think that it is OK to politically encourage kids under the age of five, compared to 5% of Lib Dems and a statistical 0% of Conservative/UKIP supporters.

The reason for left wingers' enthusiasm for getting children politically engaged at a younger age could be because they tend to be earlier political bloomers themselves. The majority of Lib Dem voters say that they had become politically aware by the age of 16, whilst the majority of Labour voters reached this point by the age of 17.

By contrast, the majority of Conservative voters reached political awareness by the age of 18, and the majority of UKIP voters weren't politically aware until the age of 20.

29 September 2016

⇨ The above information is reprinted with kind permission from YouGov. Please visit www.yougov.co.uk for further information.

The Monarch and Parliament

The Monarch visits the Houses of Parliament, usually once a year, arriving in grand style to open a new session of Parliament. This article explains more about their role.

You know who the current Monarch is? But do you know what they have to do with the UK Parliament?

The Monarch used to run the country, but not anymore

In the past Britain's kings and queens were incredibly powerful. They controlled the decisions that affected everyone in the country. Today, most of the important decisions that affect us are made by MPs and Members of the House of Lords.

It's not the UK Parliament without the Monarch

The UK Parliament has the power to pass laws for our country. It's formed of representatives from three parts: 650 MPs in the House of Commons; over 750 Members of the House of Lords; and the Monarch.

The Monarch gives 'final approval' to all laws

The Monarch signs their name to every Act of Parliament before it can become the law of the land. It would be very unusual for them to refuse.

No monarch has refused Parliament's wishes for over 300 years.

The Monarch opens Parliament every year

MPs and Lords don't meet in Parliament every day of the year. There are some breaks. It falls to the Monarch to open each new meeting – or 'session' – of Parliament. It's rather like Parliament's version of a school assembly, held for everyone, at the start of a new academic year. Take a look at 2016 State Opening photographs.

The Monarch appoints the Prime Minister after an election

The Monarch officially appoints the Prime Minister after a general election, although they don't choose the Prime Minister theirself. By tradition, they appoint the leader of the political party that wins a majority of the seats in Parliament. In 2010 there was no majority, so the Monarch appointed the leader of the party with the most seats.

When it comes to politics, the Monarch is 'neutral'

The Monarch doesn't get involved in running the Government. Nor do they publicly say what they think about political issues. This is why people sometimes say the Monarch is 'above politics'.

⇨ The above information is reprinted with kind permission from parliament.uk.

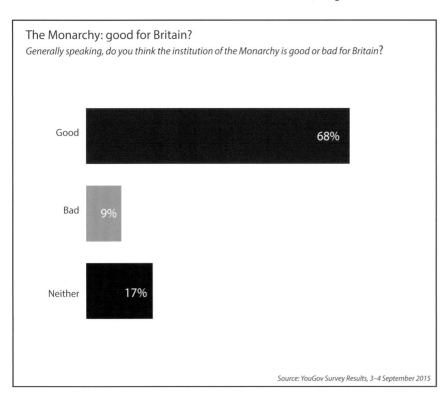

The Monarchy: good for Britain?
Generally speaking, do you think the institution of the Monarchy is good or bad for Britain?

Good — 68%
Bad — 9%
Neither — 17%

Source: YouGov Survey Results, 3–4 September 2015

How important is the monarchy to British people?

For more than 30 years, NatCen's British Social Attitudes survey has been asking the British public their views on the monarchy. The 2015 BSA report highlights important changes in attitudes towards the royal family.

First of all, regardless of when we asked, most people said having a monarchy was very important or important for the country. But the size of this majority has decreased significantly in the past 30 years. In 1983 more than four-fifths of the population (86%) were in favour of the monarchy. This figure fell to 66% in 1994 and it remained stable until 2011. This period of lower consensus coincided with allegations of Prince Charles' infidelity and his subsequent separation from Diana.

By 2011 the tide of public opinion rose again: the percentage of those who supported the monarchy reached 74% of the population. Indeed, this increase has been sustained and in 2015 almost three in four people (73%) remained in favour of the monarchy. This strong rise in support is likely to be due, in no small part, to the royal milestones that took place during this period, such as William and Kate's wedding in 2011, the Queen's Diamond Jubilee in 2012 and the birth of two Royal babies in 2013 and 2015. The high level of support in the early 1980s also followed a royal wedding and another royal baby: Prince William.

But, despite the majority declaring themselves in favour of the monarchy, support is not consistent among all groups of society. Older people were more likely to say the monarchy is important. In 2015, those who were over 55 were almost twice as likely to say this compared to those aged 17 to 24 years old. But, while older people's attitudes have remained relatively stable over time, the proportion of young people saying the monarchy is important increased from 57% to 67% between 1994 and 2015. Again, this resurgence of interest on the part of young people is likely to be thanks to the young royals such as William and Kate.

Gender seems to have an influence as well on attitudes towards the monarchy. Although between 1994 and 2011 positive opinions for both genders tended to crystallise around 65%, women always tended to be slightly more supportive. This was evident in 1983 when nine in ten women (90%) and just over four-fifths of men (83%) thought the monarchy was important. But the most significant difference was highlighted in 2015: 79% of women and 66% of men said the monarchy was important to Britain, a difference of 13 percentage points. This is probably due to some recent royal events resonating more with women than with men.

Overall, it is clear that although less of the British public considers the monarchy important than they did in 1983, on the whole we still regard the monarchy as important for our country. As the Royals' popularity seems to be enjoying a boost, are we undergoing a process of increasing trust and general satisfaction with the monarchy? Will this growth in positivity continue in the coming years? The only thing we can do is wait and see.

8 February 2016

⇨ The above information is reprinted with kind permission from NatCen Social Research. Please visit www.natcen.ac.uk for further information.

How Britain voted in 2015

For every election since 1979, Ipsos MORI has produced estimates of how the voters voted. Because the (very successful) exit poll we and GfK carry out for the BBC, ITV and Sky is only designed to predict seat shares, and by virtue of its design gives no demographic information, we hope that these figures provide a useful resource to politicians, commentators, academics and the public themselves to better understand voting behaviour, and the relative performance of the parties.

To forestall any questions, it should be noted that these are estimates, and are based on aggregating the data from our election polls and other surveys over the course of the campaign, which asked people how they intended to vote. However, as we have done in the past, the voting intention figures are weighted to the final actual results and turnout at a regional level. Whilst this means these figures are still estimates, this step should make them a more reliable guide to how different sub-groups voted (more thoughts on the performance of our polls can be found on the Ipsos MORI website, including how much of our overestimation of the Labour share may be due to Labour supporters being more likely to exaggerate their likeliness to vote, when we had other parties within two points of their actual share). The larger sample size we get from aggregating (over 9,000, including over 6,000 who said they would vote, which we hope to update later with further data to over 10,000) also allows more confidence when looking at sub-groups.

So what do the findings tell us? Here are some initial thoughts:

1. The Conservative share holds up well across most groups, as would be expected given their success in the election. Labour, meanwhile, failed to achieve the swing it needed other than among young people and renters. Labour only had a clear lead over the Conservatives among 18–34s, voters in social class DE, among private and social renters, and BME (black, minority, ethnic) voters.

2. Even worse for Labour, their vote share actually fell among those aged 65+, the highest turnout group, to just one in four. This group is where the Conservatives were most successful, gaining a 5.5 point swing from Labour since 2010. The Conservatives also achieved a three point swing from Labour among ABs, another high turnout group.

3. While the vote share of the two main parties is broadly stable, the pattern of voting for other parties has completely changed. The Liberal Democrats' vote share has collapsed across the board, only getting above 10% among ABs (their smallest fall is among those aged 65+, where they had a lower share in 2010 to begin with). They have fallen sharpest among under 34s (perhaps related to tuition fees) and private renters, who are the most likely to vote Green. Meanwhile, UKIP take third place among nearly every group (exceptions again include social classes AB, and BME voters), and do best among older, white, working class voters.

4. As we have seen in recent elections, the Conservative-Labour swing among the men and women vote overall was very similar. Both vote Conservative in relatively equal proportions, while women are slightly more likely to vote Labour and less likely to vote UKIP. There are more differences though if we do not treat men and women as homogenous groups. Most notably, younger women had the biggest swing to Labour of any group, while older women had a small swing back to the Conservatives. The two groups are almost exact opposites of each other: Labour has a 20-point lead among women aged 18–24, while the Conservatives have an 18 point lead among women over 55.

5. Both Conservatives and Labour increased their vote share among BME voters, but remained unchanged among white voters. This may be related to the rise of UKIP among white voters (to 14% of the vote), which may have cancelled out some of the Liberal Democrat's fall, while among BME voters only 2% said they would vote UKIP.

6. Patterns of turnout remain relatively unchanged, with concerning implications for the future of democratic engagement. There appears to be no significant increase in turnout among young people, with 18–24s almost half as likely to vote as those aged 65% (43% vs 78%; in 2010 estimated turnout for 18–24s was 44%). Similarly, turnout remains lower among the working classes, renters, and BME communities.

26 August 2015

⇨ The above information is reprinted with kind permission from Ipsos MORI. Please visit www.ipsos-mori.com for further information.

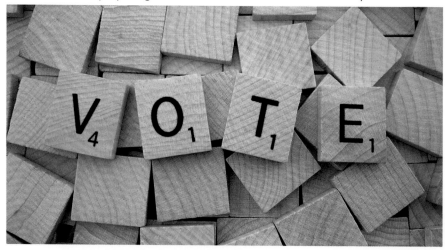

Digital democracy and opportunities for a 21st-century Parliament

Designing for Democracy is the Crick Centre's major research and public engagement project, exploring the planned restoration and renewal of the Palace of Westminster. In this blog, the latest in our Designing for Democracy series, Victoria Boelman examines how the restoration offers opportunities for a 21st-century Parliament.

"At the moment, simply getting WiFi access is an achievement in some parts of Parliament"

With the recommendation this autumn that the restoration of the Palace of Westminster should go ahead, temporarily relocating both Houses elsewhere in Westminster, a tantalising prospect has been opened up. The report by the Restoration and Renewal Parliamentary Committee declared that a core objective, alongside fixing the roof, wiring and plumbing, is to ensure the Palace is fit for "the needs of a 21st-century Parliament for (i) the public, and (ii) Parliamentarians".

"As with all engagement, the key is to consider who is being engaged, why and when"

This should be an exciting proposition. What do we, the citizens of the United Kingdom want our new and improved Parliament to be? Obviously we are working within the constraints of a UNESCO World Heritage site but that is not to say we cannot make some modifications to the design and layout or, perhaps more significantly, change the practices of Parliament. How can this opportunity be used to improve working practices, increase citizen engagement, restore trust in politics, and improve the quality and legitimacy of decision-making?

At Nesta we are excited about two opportunities to do this. The first is to say "What if we just experiment?". For several years MPs, Peers, staff and all those who interact with them will have no choice but to do things differently. So rather than just 'making do' or 'muddling through', what would happen if we took the chance to actively try out some new ways of working that we might want to take back into the restored Palace? There are myriad examples of things we could try, from less adversarial seating arrangements (as already modelled in the Welsh Assembly and Scottish Parliament) to greater public access (citizens in Australia have access to around 20% of their Parliament building, compared to around 10% in the UK), to capitalising on the potential of new technologies to open up our democratic processes, making them more transparent and engaging for everyone. As the plans for the big move progress, we'll be talking more about how the temporary Houses could become Living Labs for democracy.

And that leads on to the second big opportunity – the role of digital technologies. At the moment, simply getting WiFi access is an achievement in some parts of Parliament. With all that set to change, what can we do differently? We have been investigating pioneers of digital democracy across the globe, trying to understand what works, the challenges and opportunities. Two areas are proving particularly popular on the international stage – the crowdsourcing of policy, and greater collaboration on the development of legislation. For example, many countries are experimenting with ways of enabling citizen-led initiatives to reach Parliament for debate and potentially passing into law. One example is the Rahvaalgatus (Estonian People's Assembly) which has seen three new items of legislation adopted since 2013, with another four partially adopted and more under discussion. In France, Parlement & Citoyens is designed "to connect deputies and senators who wish to involve citizens in the preparation of their legislative proposals". These new platforms encourage debate and deliberation and voting to determine which to pursue further. Further afield, Pol.is, a tool which visualises consensus and agreement in a debate, has been used to inform the development of new regulation of Uber in Taiwan, and in Brazil the House of Deputies has its own in-house Hacker Lab which develops tools for public participation in the legislative process, via its e-Democracia portal.

Of course, it is not easy. The UK has already experimented with a Public Reading Stage of new Bills, with the aim of increasing engagement at the final stage of the legislative process. It was not a great success. As with all engagement, the key is to consider who is being engaged, why and when. Impenetrable legal jargon and lengthy documents are all off-putting and so this may not have been the place to start. But when the outcomes are more tangible and the knowledge of citizens as experts in their lives and that of their community is more valuable, then it can be worth the investment. Which brings me to my last point – digital must become an integral part of the way our Parliament works but it must not be seen as a cheap substitute for other forms of engagement. It takes time and effort to make sure that engagement is inclusive and representative, and that applies as much, if not more so, to digital. The most successful approaches are those which combine offline and online methods to encourage participation from people from all walks of life, which must surely be the ultimate aim of any 21st-century Parliament.

24 October 2016

⇨ The above information is reprinted with kind permission from The Crick Centre. Please visit www.crickcentre.org for further information.

Three things that must happen for devolution to be a success: economic development, revenue generation and democracy

If devolution is to be a success, argues Rachel Laurence, those who control devolution policy must ensure that it stimulates the kind of economic development that will improve the prosperity of all communities within the devolved areas, generates greater levels and control of revenue and capital for regional government, and creates meaningful democratic structures.

The leader of Birmingham city council this week argued for the creation of a "West Midlands sovereign wealth fund" – an idea that would see money raised from local government pension funds invested in housing and other local projects.

It's exciting to see proposals like this that seek to tackle shortfalls in public infrastructure and housing investment, through creative long-term use of public sector assets. Using assets as a way to generate long-term revenue appears to be a much more efficient use of resources, than selling them off outright.

It also provides an opportunity for local communities to have a much more direct connection, as citizens represented by local government, both to how investment is prioritised, and how revenue is re-spent, than they do when major infrastructure investment is led purely by the private sector.

From our regular engagement with people working to improve local economies across the UK, it's clear there's an eagerness to connect their community focussed strategies into the regional level of economic development.

But there's a recurring problem that the priorities of local communities – be it individuals' prosperity, a more democratic decision-making process or the sustainable use of resources – don't match up with the regional pursuit to rapidly increase their national growth contribution.

It must be possible to not just overlay regional and city growth strategies with the kinds of socio-economic outcomes that matter most to communities, but to design regional economic strategies that deliver good community level economic outcomes in the first place.

Today we launch a new paper that argues devolution – done properly – offers an opportunity to pursue a new kind of regional economic development, and a new kind of economic governance.

But to make good on this promise, it has to be better equipped to do three crucial things:

1. Stimulate the kind of economic development that will improve the prosperity of all communities within the devolved areas

Economic strategies that seek primarily to increase a region's contribution to national growth, as measured through 'gross value added' (GVA) – focus on the production of goods and services – usually, high-end growth industries – and the infrastructure or business support that facilitates this.

Yet these strategies do not necessarily help achieve any of the following objectives: a more equal distribution of wealth across the population; greater diversity of small and large businesses or sectors; high local investment from money spent in a local economy; strong flow of local population through local education and training into local jobs.

Rather than pursue those aims separately, through training and skills, business development or poverty-reduction programmes, they could be much more efficiently tackled if they were treated as an integral part of the regional economic strategy itself.

2. Generate greater levels and control of revenue and capital for regional government

Current devolution agreements see retention of tight central controls over the grants paid to new combined local authorities, as well as over the levels of borrowing they are permitted.

This undermines the possibility of new, larger urban authorities being able to use any expansion of their tax base – for example through new powers to retain business rates – as leverage for ambitious regional development plans, paid for initially through borrowing. To fulfil many of the promises of devolution, some further relaxation of borrowing requirements, matched by greater flexibility in setting local tax rates, is crucial.

3. Create meaningful democratic structures

Democracy is a missing link in the new devolution debate. It is essential that the Department for Communities and Local Government (DCLG) and groups of local authorities proposing devolution deals consider how to engage citizens and increase accountability, especially with deals being made on an ad hoc basis and the role of elected members at each level varying from place to place.

Clearer accountability structures would show where responsibility lies between combined authorities, local authorities and central government, and how citizens can hold each set of leaders to account. More meaningful structures for citizen participation could be built into the design and delivery of services, and the development of strategic visions and budget-setting, with clear channels of influence to policy-making and accountability ties to representative institutions.

This would enable us to move away from the current situation where central government, which is supposed to be transferring power away from itself, paradoxically ends up with more power because of its role in granting concessions and monitoring devolution agreements.

Aspiring for an approach to devolution that does this is not wishful thinking. Devolution deals that fail to deliver on these aims risk moving our economy, and governance structures, in the opposite direction. We will be building on this body of work examining devolution from a number of angles, over the next year, so keep an eye out for more.

9 February 2016

⇨ The above information is reprinted with kind permission from The Crick Centre. Please visit www.crickcentre.org for further information.

A three-minute guide: what is the EU?

Introduction

The UK's membership of the European Union has long divided public opinion. With an in/out referendum scheduled for 23 June, voters will be tasked with making a decision that will shape the country's future relationship with Europe. But what is the EU? And how does it function in practice?

What is the EU?

The European Union (EU) is an economic and political partnership between 28 countries. The EU is unique – it is not a state, and yet it is more than an international organisation such as the United Nations.

Member states cooperate on issues ranging from the single market to defence and foreign policy. Particularly in areas of economic policy, such as trade, national governments have ceded some authority in favour of joint decision-making, and the adoption of binding EU-wide laws.

How did it develop?

The European Union has evolved over the past 70 years. The European Coal and Steel Community (ECSC) was formed in 1951 with the aim of binding Germany and France together in a trading alliance and preventing future wars. The European Atomic Energy Community was created in 1957 to foster cooperation in nuclear energy. The European Economic Community was established in the same year with the broader remit of economic integration. The three organisations were merged in 1965 and referred to as the "European Communities". They were subsumed within the new "European Union" in 1992, when the Maastricht Treaty was agreed.

Britain has always had a strained relationship with these organisations. It declined an invitation to join the six founding members of the ECSC in 1957 – even though British politicians, notably Winston Churchill, favoured the close integration of European states and championed initiatives aimed at international cooperation in Europe. Britain twice attempted to join the European Economic Community in the 1960s, but its applications were vetoed by France. It finally joined in 1973, along with Denmark and Ireland, but held a national referendum on membership two years later. 67% voted to stay in, 33% opposed.

What are the EU's institutions?

The EU has several key institutions that were created by national governments to help them achieve the goals that they set out in the founding treaties. Checks and balances were built into the system to prevent any single body or member state from imposing its preferences unilaterally.

These institutions are at the heart of the EU system, but national institutions also play key roles. Governments attend the European Council and the Council of the European Union, administrations and agencies implement and enforce EU policy, national parliaments are consulted during the decision-making process, and parliaments and courts contribute to accountability and scrutiny. The combination of EU and national institutions distinguishes the EU from other international organisations.

⇨ The European Council is the most senior EU institution. It consists of the elected heads of the member states, and is accountable through national parliaments to national populations. It sets the EU's general political direction and handles sensitive issues. It sometimes calls on the other institutions to draft legislative proposals on a particular subject.

⇨ The European Commission combines political and administrative responsibilities. It is in charge of implementing legislation and monitoring compliance by the member states. Its most important task is to formulate policy proposals, which it forwards to the Council of the EU and the European Parliament. It employs around 33,000 people, and is based in Brussels (in contrast, the British civil service employs around half a million). Each member state nominates one member, who then serves (independently) as the "Commissioner" responsible for a certain department. Recently, the UK's Commissioners have run the EU's trade (Lord Mandelson) and financial services portfolios (Lord Hill). The Commission sits for five-year terms, and is usually referred to by the name of its president (hence, we currently have the "Juncker Commission").

⇨ The Council of the European Union is the main body for the representation of member states' interests, where national ministers meet to negotiate and agree on legislation, supported by national civil servants who handle more technical aspects. Decisions are taken by ministers in their area of responsibility. For example, when agriculture is discussed, the farming ministers attend, and so on. The Council shares the power to decide with the European Parliament whether to adopt proposals made by the Commission.

⇨ The European Parliament is the EU's directly elected chamber. It consists of 751 MEPs, drawn from all the member states. There are currently 73 British MEPs. In the May 2014 election UKIP won 24 MEPs, Labour won 20, the Conservatives won 19, the Greens won three, SNP won two, and the Liberal Democrats, Plaid Cymru, Sinn Fein, Democratic Unionists, and Ulster Unionists each won one seat. However, MEPs sit in European parliamentary groups rather than as national delegations. For example, Conservative MEPs sit in the European Conservatives and Reformists (ECR) group, while Labour MEPs sit in the Socialists and Democrats (S&D) group. The two largest political groups are the centre-right European People's Party (EPP) and the centre-left S&D group.

The main power of the European Parliament is to take decisions on EU legislation with the member state governments in the Council. The Parliament shares control of the EU budget with the European Council, ratifies international treaties, oversees the work of the Commission, and elects the Commission (after each European election). The Parliament also has the power to sack the Commission, by a two-thirds majority vote.

How does the EU make law?

For most legislation, the process starts with a proposal by the Commission, which is sent to the Parliament and the Council for their consideration. The Parliament and the Council can each decide to amend, approve or reject a proposal. For any proposal to become law, it has to be agreed by both institutions. EU citizens are represented in this process by their MEPs in the Parliament and their ministers in the Council.

Once the Council and Parliament have both agreed a text it becomes law, and passes to national governments to implement, overseen by the Commission and the Court of Justice. EU laws can take two forms. The most common form – EU directives – are the "softer" version: they specify what should be done, but leave how to the member states. This means that member states have to pass national legislation to bring it into effect. Regulations, in contrast, apply directly. There is no additional process at the national level and no room for national interpretation.

Produced by The UK in a Changing Europe.

⇨ The above information is reprinted with kind permission from The UK in a Changing Europe. Please visit www.ukandeu.ac.uk for further information.

© The UK in a Changing Europe 2017

What is Brexit?

What is Brexit? Brexit means that the UK will leave the EU. Brexit means that the UK will no longer be a member of the EU. That is what Brexit is. And there the clarity and confidence ends.

By Stephen Weatherill, the Jacques Delors Professor of European Law at Oxford University.

The UK post-Brexit will join the group of over 160 states across the world which are not members of the EU. It would be an exaggeration to claim that there are over 160 models governing the relationship between states that are not members of the EU and the EU, but not by much. There is a wide spectrum, stretching from states with an intimate relationship with the EU involving acceptance of large chunks of the EU's legislative acquis; through states which possess a free trade agreement with the EU (these take several forms); states whose relationship with the EU is based on the WTO but adorned by extra sectoral deals; states which relate on the basis of the WTO alone; and, at the far extreme, pariah states with no engagement in multilateral deal-making.

So the UK will ultimately be located somewhere on this spectrum, stretching from Norway to North Korea. That is what Brexit is.

Brexit, then, involves choices: choices made by the UK, choices made by the EU-27. The key choices that need to be made are readily divided into three types: the external, the UK–EU and the internal.

External

This concerns most of all the scope and nature of the UK's trade policy with the rest of the world. Some Brexiteers have painted a picture of the post-Brexit UK pursuing rapid and fruitful negotiations with major economic powers round the world, and arriving at deals tailored to the UK's particular interests and strengths. Leaving aside sceptical questions about the plausibility of the timetable and the incentives of these major powers to dedicate resources to negotiating with a state that has just abandoned the most sophisticated multilateral trading bloc the world has ever seen, there is a key choice that must be made before any such vision may be implemented. That choice is – will the UK stay in the EU's customs union, or not? If it does, that ability to pursue an external trade policy independent of the EU's is surrendered. But if it does not, goods and services made or marketed in the UK will face high and costly barriers to entry into the EU's market.

UK–EU

The choice here asks, in short, how much of the EU's body of rules will the UK choose to adopt and follow in order to secure privileged access to the EU's internal market. The EU's internal market does not possess a precise economic or legal definition – rather, it is a political construct that has evolved incrementally over time. It is, however, marked by a high degree of commitment to the 'four freedoms' – free movement of goods, (natural and legal) persons, services and capital – plus a highly developed competition policy supported by a relatively dense set of common policies agreed over time on obvious trade-related matters, such as product standards, but also in the areas of labour market regulation, consumer protection, environmental standards, and so on. It is conceivable that the UK will be able to cut a deal involving some degree of autonomy from the full complexity of the legislative acquis governing the EU's internal market in exchange for some degree of privileged access to that internal market. It is not conceivable that the UK will be allowed to cherry-pick what it sees as the benefits of a post-Brexit relationship with the EU-27 and resist what it sees as burdens. Choices will need to be made about how far, if at all, the UK is willing to go in aligning its laws with those of the EU-27.

Internal

It is commonly stated that the UK's departure from the EU will immediately cause a legislative and administrative task on an immense scale, as the UK chooses which EU-sourced rules it will abandon, which it will amend and which it will continue to apply. It is certainly true that there will arise a whole host of choices. Labour market regulation, consumer protection, environmental law, the grant of aid to industry, and competition law are all examples of areas where there is currently a partial or, in some instances, total overlay of EU rules. In fact it is not easy to think of any significant area of law or policy in the UK which is not in some way 'Europeanised'.

Withdraw from the EU, and a state may make its own choices about such matters, but if it tries to start with a clean slate it will be doing nothing else apart from writing on it for years to come, as it re-invents its regulatory scheme. But in fact the job need not be so brutally taxing. Once a deal is done (if a deal is done) with the EU on the basic shape of withdrawal, it would be perfectly straightforward to repeal the statutes which form the 'bridge' across which EU law travels to reach the UK's legal order, but at the same time to legislate that all measures that have been made over time pursuant to the obligations imposed by EU membership shall continue in force in the UK notwithstanding Brexit. There would be no change of substance at all. And the practical point would be that it could be considered at leisure and over time which of these measures should be retained, which changed and which abrogated. There is no rush in making the choices.

Clearly there are interconnections between the three groups of choices: most of all, the more intimate the relationship the UK wishes to pursue with the EU-27 (choice 2), the less flexibility it will enjoy in making choices 1 and 3. 'Hard' Brexit means (roughly) surrendering the economic advantages of privileged access to the internal market – choice 2 – in order to maximise the perceived scope for external and internal action that is free of the influence of the EU – choices 1 and 3. 'Soft' Brexit, by contrast, is heavily conditioned by a desire to secure that privileged market access and a consequent readiness to absorb much of the EU's body of rules even as the UK quits the EU, even if that has a cost measured in reduced external and internal scope for unilateral action.

None of these choices has been made.

Different Brexiteers have made very different claims at different times about which model they favour, sometimes making perfectly irreconcilable claims about the choices they prefer. Now they have to choose. And once they have chosen, and once the blood has been wiped from the floor after the intense political battles that will be fought over the choosing, they will need to take these choices to the EU and see what they can negotiate.

Whatever choice is made will not be backed by a mandate supplied by June's referendum. The Leave campaign chose not to put one particular vision of Brexit before the voters. This was understandable. They could not have delivered a single vision without exposing the enormity of the gap between, on the one hand, the Leavers who want to maintain a high level of privileged access to the EU's internal market while hoping to reduce the UK's exposure to the full range of accompanying regulatory obligations (especially concerning the free movement of persons) and, on the other, the Leavers who were eager to skip free of the EU's embrace entirely in pursuit of a vision of global trade on terms tailored to the UK's needs alone. And the Leave campaign's evasion of the choices allowed it to assemble a much wider group of supporters than would have been possible had it made the choices and pinned down one particular model of Brexit in advance of the referendum.

Strategically it was a brilliantly successful way to win the referendum. Choices that were not made – choices that were calculatedly evaded – are choices that now must be made. To insist that whatever deal is finally struck with the EU-27 should be subject to the approval of the British people is not to countermand the verdict delivered last June: it is instead to ensure that verdict be arrived at on the basis of production of all the evidence. If this means that Brexit is a process not an event – a neverendum rather than a referendum – then that is simply the consequence of the way that the Leave campaign chose not to choose what Brexit is. The mandate they have for Brexit is incomplete. Because 'What Brexit is' is still not clear.

⇨ The above information is reprinted with kind permission from The UK in a Changing Europe. Please visit www.ukandeu.ac.uk for further information.

Referendums held in the UK

A referendum is a method of referring a question or set of questions to the entire electorate directly.

Since 1973 there have been 11 referendums held in the UK, the majority of them have been related to the issue of devolution. The first UK-wide referendum was held in 1975 on the United Kingdom's continued membership of the European Community (European Union).

EU referendum 2016

A referendum on the UK's membership of the European Union took place on 23 June 2016, when the UK voted to leave the EU. For information about the result and the process for leaving the EU, see the House of Commons Library EU referendum pages via parliament.uk.

Previous referendums in the UK

⇨ 8 March 1973: Northern Ireland – Northern Ireland sovereignty referendum on whether Northern Ireland should remain part of the United Kingdom or join the Republic of Ireland (yes to remaining part of the UK)

⇨ 5 June 1975: UK – Membership of the European Community referendum on whether the UK should stay in the European Community (yes)

⇨ 1 March 1979: Scotland – Scottish devolution referendum on whether there should be a Scottish Assembly (40 per cent of the electorate had to vote yes in the referendum, although a small majority voted yes this was short of the 40 per cent threshold required to enact devolution)

⇨ 1 March 1979: Wales – Welsh devolution referendum on whether there should be a Welsh Assembly (no)

⇨ 11 September 1997: Scotland – Scottish devolution referenda on whether there should be a Scottish Parliament and whether the Scottish Parliament should have tax varying powers (both referendums received a yes vote)

⇨ 18 September 1997: Wales – Welsh devolution referendum on whether there should be a National Assembly for Wales (yes)

⇨ 7 May 1998: London – Greater London Authority referendum on whether there should be a Mayor of London and Greater London Authority (yes)

⇨ 22 May 1998: Northern Ireland – Northern Ireland Belfast Agreement referendum on the Good Friday Agreement (yes)

⇨ 3 March 2011: Wales – Welsh devolution referendum on whether the National Assembly for Wales should gain the power to legislate on a wider range of matters (yes)

⇨ 5 May 2011: UK – referendum on whether to change the voting system for electing MPs to the House of Commons from first past the post to the alternative vote (no, first past the post will continue to be used to elect MPs to the House of Commons)

⇨ 18 September 2014: Scotland – referendum on whether Scotland should become an independent country (no, the electorate voted 55 per cent to 45 per cent in favour of Scotland remaining within the UK).

⇨ The above information is reprinted with kind permission from Parliament UK. Please visit www.parliament.uk for further information.

Britain is leaving the EU – will other countries follow?

By Simon Usherwood, Senior Lecturer in Politics, University of Surrey

The British decision to leave the EU has been a long time in the making, but it does not lessen the shock that many politicians in the UK and across the EU are feeling.

While London begins the long process of negotiating an exit from the European Union, some of our attention must now turn to the rest of the organisation and to the other member states.

Even though the UK has been an outlier, in terms of its attitudes towards the EU, it is far from alone in harbouring people who want to change the direction and nature of the union. The ultimate success of the long-running British campaign to secure exit will have given succour to counterparts elsewhere to continue and redouble their efforts.

To some extent, eurosceptics outside the UK have an easier time of things. The use of proportional representation means it has been much easier for them to gain seats in national parliaments. And because vocal eurosceptics are to be found right across the European political spectrum, they have a relatively good chance of making it into a coalition government. They come from the right, the left and even the centre ground, and they already occupy positions of power in Denmark, Finland and Poland.

Citizens in many European countries are also far more used to voting in referendums than the British, leaving their governments in a bind.

As the British debate has shown, it is very hard to argue a case against "giving the people a voice", especially while the EU continues to look so weak in its response to the refugee crisis and the continuing failings of the eurozone.

Populists across the continent have seen the EU as both a symbol and a direct cause of what ails their countries. They have found it a particularly convenient target for blame when it comes to austerity and immigration.

After all, the EU is poorly placed to defend itself and there are very few people at the national level willing to devote political capital to shielding it.

The end of the EU?

However, this desire to continue attacking the EU does not necessarily mean others will follow Britain out of the EU.

For one thing, the shock of the British vote is likely to concentrate a lot of minds. No longer merely an irritant, euroscepticism is now a clear and present threat to the union's future development. That means ignoring or trivialising the problem looks less and less viable as a strategy.

Quite how the EU can engage with eurosceptics is not clear. It has not had a huge amount of success at becoming more democratic, despite good intentions. The best way to start is to build from a willingness to try to debate the issues. Eurosceptics might not have the answers to the EU's woes, but they ask many of the right questions.

The British case is also likely to demonstrate the costs of exit much more graphically than any speech ever could. With a strong consensus from economists that the UK is now about to take a hit to its bottom line in the coming months, this might well give eurosceptics elsewhere second thoughts. This will only be strengthened by the likely desire of governments to offer the UK a less-than-generous deal, precisely so as to head off domestic demands.

Of course, in the longer term if it does prove that the UK is better off outside the EU, then this can only be bad for those same governments and good for eurosceptics. The threat of economic ruin will recede and everyone will have to recalibrate their understanding of the benefits of membership. However, this is something that will not become evident for several years at least.

And this brings us to the final logic: the UK is different.

> ## "Any eurozone country that voted to leave the EU would find that the resulting need to reintroduce its national currency would cause huge economic outflows"

As was rightly pointed out during the campaign, the UK had a number of opt-outs from various EU policies, including the Schengen system of free movement, justice and home affairs and, most importantly, the euro. No other member state has such a degree of latitude.

This matters because the more a country is entangled in the EU, the harder it is to leave. Euro membership in particular is a degree of entanglement far beyond what the UK had.

Any eurozone country that voted to leave the EU would find that the resulting need to reintroduce its national currency would cause huge economic outflows (by those worried about a loss in value during any subsequent conversion process) that would dwarf anything we will see for the UK. With no easy solution to this problem, those who might push for an exit from the EU might feel that the cost is simply too high.

However, such practicalities are not the point, at least not at this stage. There is now a scalp that eurosceptics from all countries can claim in support of their cause. They will now be looking for their next one.

24 June 2016

⇨ The above information is reprinted with kind permission from *The Conversation*. Please visit www.theconversation.com for further information.

Brexit: what happens next?

Following the victory for Leave in the EU referendum, Professor Stephen Tierney sets out the next steps in the constitutional process.

Initially nothing: the referendum by itself does not change anything in legal terms. The UK remains a member of the European Union until it concludes negotiations on withdrawal, a process that will take at least two years.

Two-year negotiation: under the Treaty of European Union, states have a specific right to withdraw from the EU. The United Kingdom must go through a process set out by Article 50 of the Treaty. The UK Government will give notice (we don't know when) to the other European heads of government – the European Council – that the UK intends to leave. The UK will then negotiate the terms of its departure over a two-year period; an extension of this period is possible.

"The EU does not want to introduce a pick-and-mix arrangement that could encourage other Member States to unsettle an increasingly fragile union"

If agreement is reached by the UK and 20 of the other 28 Council members (this is the majority required), then that will be formalised. If negotiations do not conclude in agreement, the UK can still leave at the end of this period, although the terms of this departure may not be favourable to the UK.

There are various options that could be concluded. One of course is complete exclusion of the UK from any of the EU's treaty arrangements. That would seem to be very unlikely. Once the dust settles it is clear that Europe would benefit from a suitable trade deal with the UK and vice versa. But this is all for discussion and will depend upon the political mood, particularly among other EU states.

Delaying negotiations: the negotiations need not happen straight away. It would make sense for the UK Government to plan this carefully and for a full internal discussion to take place across the parties and the territories of the UK to try to build consensus as to what the UK's negotiating position should be. The EU and other Member States kept a fairly low profile during the campaign, so it is hard to predict what European reactions will be; it is also important to distinguish public statements from private, diplomatic positions.

Can it all be stopped? The referendum result is not legally binding and the PM could simply refuse to notify the EU of an intention to leave. In political terms this is unthinkable (the PM has in any case announced his impending resignation), as is any attempt by Parliament to try to block the negotiations.

Will a deal be done? There are many reasons to believe that in the end both sides will come to an arrangement that sees the UK still connected to the EU in a range of ways. These are:

⇨ the importance of trade (the UK is a key importer of European goods);

⇨ the significance to the EU of the UK's international status, strategic position, territorial waters and natural resources;

⇨ the number of citizens of the EU living in the UK and vice versa;

⇨ the EU's direction of travel: trade deals with external partners are proliferating, for example with the countries of North America.

But there are potentially huge stumbling blocks: the EU does not want to introduce a pick-and-mix arrangement that could encourage other Member States to unsettle an increasingly fragile union.

There are other complications. For example, the UK's membership of the WTO is currently dependent upon EU membership, so that will also have to be untangled.

Staying in the European Union? The result was a relatively close one: 52%–48%. Could the negotiation deal lead to the UK staying in the EU on very different terms?

"There are many known unknowns, most of which are political questions which will hinge on how things play out"

There are legal impediments to the Article 50 process being used to renegotiate terms, but the EU does not let legal niceties get in the way of realpolitik when the stakes are high. Some believe that the EU did not want to reveal its hand before the referendum, but may now offer better terms of membership to the UK. Brexit is a headache it could do without. UK 'leavers' would have to be brought onside, but many of these are 'soft-leavers'. The referendum did not offer a mid-way option – a reformed EU, or a better position for the UK within it – beyond the deal negotiated by the Prime Minister. There was no promise of a 'Smith Commission' to appease those who want reform. Will the EU try to bring about such a reform? The UK is so embedded within the EU that untangling membership would be a massive task that may in time appear unnecessary.

There is of course a strong argument that this simply won't happen. Such an accommodation of the UK would surely need treaty reform and would therefore require the unanimous consent of all Member States to any new deal. As I say, it would also open the door for other states to push for reform and better terms. This latter point could well mean that, for Brussels and the dominant forces within the EU, the political cost could just be too high; the danger being that the monetary union itself could collapse. But this issue will be on the table when the dust settles, and over time the gap between a free trade deal for the UK and ongoing membership may start to shrink towards vanishing point.

Parliament's role: Westminster would still have a significant role to play in offering views in negotiations and in ratifying the exit Treaty (or refusing to do so).

"The referendum result is not legally binding and the PM could simply refuse to notify the EU of an intention to leave"

Because of the power Parliament has ultimately to accept or reject a deal, it would also expect to be kept closely informed. This will be a period for parliamentarians to show their mettle, calling the UK negotiators to account, and making sure the people of the UK are as fully-informed as possible. Transparency has not been a characteristic of EU treaty-making and it will be for the Commons and the Lords to insist upon this. It will also be vital for the Scottish Parliament and other devolved legislatures to feed into this process and to scrutinise it energetically.

The possibility of another General Election (and devolved elections) before an exit treaty is agreed should not be discounted. Europe would obviously be a major issue in these elections and the results of any elections could impact upon negotiating positions.

In the meantime: the UK remains a Member State of the EU and fully subject to its obligations under EU law. This means that is very difficult (in reality impossible) to change any of the current arrangements regarding free movement, etc. until the UK has concluded its exit treaty. There can be no immediate ban on free movement of EU citizens for example.

Massive job for law-makers: Parliament must also reform UK law. A significant claim of the Leave campaign was the extent to which EU law has been incorporated into UK law. This will all have to be revised – a major headache for legislators and for government civil servants.

There is another point. So big is this task that it will have to take priority over much else, clogging up the parliamentary timetable and presumably putting on hold much of the programme in the last Queen's Speech. Will there be parliamentary space to take forward the new Wales Bill, reforming Welsh devolution, for example? EU exit will also no doubt preoccupy the devolved legislatures and governments, impacting significantly on the process of government in Scotland, Wales and Northern Ireland over the next few years.

Implications for the Union? Already Scottish nationalists and Irish nationalists in Northern Ireland have made the point that this is not a popular decision in their territories, and that they will oppose exit. Calls for a second referendum on independence in Scotland may intensify, as could calls for a referendum under the Northern Ireland Act 1998 for reunification of Ireland. It is not clear that opposition to Brexit will translate automatically into majority support for Scottish independence (and far less likely for Irish reunification): does Scotland want to be the site of the EU's territorial border with England? But the devolved territories will offer strong views throughout the negotiation process, and the prospect of Scottish independence may well push the UK towards trying to retain an integrated relationship with the EU.

The Scotland Act 2016 strengthens Scotland's position in a 'federal' direction; strengthening the constitutional status of the Scottish Parliament as a firm partner in the Union. An exit treaty could possibly be pushed through Westminster without the Scottish Parliament's consent. But this would go against the spirit of the 2016 Act and of devolution as a whole. It could also lead to court challenges, which even if unsuccessful would sour relations between London and Edinburgh in a highly toxic way. The need to carry the devolved territories along in any negotiation process is crucial to the health of the UK. It would be ironic if the UK were to secure its 'independence' from Europe, only then to fall apart as a state.

Northern Ireland is possibly an even more serious issue than Scotland. The peace process has largely been a success, and a main plank in the thawing of relations across the island of Ireland has been the Common Travel Area between the UK and the Republic of Ireland. It is vital that the slow growth in closer relations across Ireland should not be jeopardised. This is arguably the most important issue for exit negotiations, particularly if there is any question that the peace process is at stake.

Points of uncertainty: these could fill a book…

There are many known unknowns, most of which are political questions which will hinge on how things play out.

⇨ What will this mean for the Conservative Party and the Government? The PM has announced he will resign within the next few months. Where do we go from here?

⇨ What will it mean for Europe? Will other states now seek to reform the EU from within? Will other exit movements across the Continent grow in strength?

⇨ Will the EU try to see off exit by offering the UK a new deal? If so, would the UK Government be politically able to negotiate a settlement short of exit?

⇨ What will it mean for the UK economy and indeed for the economies of our European partners, for the pound and the euro?

It is not a time for predictions. We must wait and see…

24 June 2016

⇨ The above information is reprinted with kind permission from the Centre on Constitutional Change. Please visit www.centreonconstitutionalchange.ac.uk for further information.

Key facts

⇨ In 2015, 118,100 foreign citizens naturalised as British citizens. This is down more than 40% from 2013, when citizenship grants reached almost 208,000, the largest annual number since records began in 1962. (page 6)

⇨ From 2009 to 2013, citizenship grants averaged 195,800 per year. (page 6)

⇨ The number of decisions made on citizenship applications in 2015 did not increase in line with an increase in the number of applications submitted (applications increased by about 23,700 or 18% from 2014 to 2015), suggesting that the declining trend in citizenship grants may end in 2016 as these applications are processed. (page 6)

⇨ Proposals for the "first nation state in space" have been unveiled by a team of scientists and legal experts, who say the move will foster peace, open up access to space technologies and offer protection for citizens of planet Earth. (page 14)

⇨ 73% of Nigerians feel they are global citizens, compared to 71% in china, 70% in Peru and 67% in India. (page 18)

⇨ Young people, here 18- to 21-year-olds, are less engaged in traditional, electoral politics (especially voting) than the general population, but as engaged in other forms of participation. Those in education are more active than the general population in all forms of participation except voting and contact (although the gap here is not that large) and have higher levels of social and political trust. (page 21)

⇨ 18- to 21-year-olds in higher education have similar levels of engagement in electoral politics as the mean figure for all ages, but are much more likely to engage in all other forms of participation than the general population. They also have higher levels of social and political trust than the general population and are much more likely to sign petitions, participate in demonstrations and join boycotts than 18-21 year olds not in higher education. (page 21)

⇨ Being in education boosts participation for 18–21s in almost all political acts, especially for those from low income backgrounds, who actually outperform those from high income backgrounds in education for working for an organisation or association, signing a petition, going on a demonstration, or participating in a boycott. It also shows that 18- to 21-year-olds in education from low income backgrounds outperform those from high income backgrounds who are not

in education on these measures, as well as being significantly more likely to vote. (page 21)

⇨ People who volunteer in sport have a 10% higher self-esteem, emotional wellbeing and resilience than those who have never volunteered. (page 22)

⇨ Those who have never volunteered in sport are more likely to feel unhappy, sad or depressed. (page 22)

⇨ A high proportion of first-generation migrants (born abroad) believe in the duty to vote. (page 25)

⇨ In England 4% of councillors, candidates and MPs who come from an ethnic minority. In Wales it is 0.8% and in Scotland the percentage of non-white councillors is similar to that of its population at 3.4%. (page 25)

⇨ Nearly a quarter of Labour (24%) and Lib Dem (23%) voters think it is appropriate to have started politically encouraging a child by the age of ten (compared to 10% of Conservatives and 8% of Ukippers). (page 27)

⇨ Most people say having a monarchy is very important or important for the country. But the size of this majority has decreased significantly in the past 30 years. In 1983 more than four-fifths of the population (86%) were in favour of the monarchy. This figure fell to 66% in 1994 and it remained stable until 2011. (page 29)

⇨ In 2015: 79% of women and 66% of men said the monarchy was important to Britain, a difference of 13 percentage points. (page 29)

Brexit

An abbreviation that stands for 'British exit'. Referring to the referendum that took place on 23 June 2016 where British citizens voted to exit the European Union.

Citizenship

A citizen is an inhabitant of a city, town or country. The concept of citizenship indicates that a person feels as though they are a member of the society in which they live, and that they conduct themselves in a way that is responsible and respectful to fellow citizens.

Citizenship (education)

Unesco defines citizenship education as: educating children, from early childhood, to become clear-thinking and enlightened citizens who participate in decisions concerning society. 'Society' is here understood in the special sense of a nation with a circumscribed territory which is recognized as a state.

Ethnic minority

A group of people who are different in their ancestry, culture and traditions from the majority of the population.

European Union (EU)

The European Union (EU) is a group of countries, whose governments work together to improve the way people live in Europe. It was formed in 1957, with just six members, and has grown to include 27 countries. In order to become members, countries are required to pay money (usually in the form of taxes) and agree to follow a set of rules/guidelines.

Global citizen

Someone who places their identity within the global community rather than their own country/nation.

Government

UK Government is responsible for managing the country. Our Government decides how our taxes are spent, and there are different departments that run different things; the Department of Health, the Department of Education, etc. UK Government is run by the political party with the greatest representation in the House of Commons and is led by the Prime Minister.

Immigration

To immigrate is to move permanently from your home country, and settle somewhere else.

Manifesto

A manifesto is usually produced by a political party, and sets out their policy, beliefs and aims in a public document.

Monarchy

A Monarchy is a form of government that has a monarch as the head of state.

Multiculturalism

A number of different cultures coexisting side-by-side, for example within a school or a country.

Nationalism

Nationalism is often considered to be more aggressive than patriotism, implying the desire to be a completely separate nation and intolerance of influences from other cultures. For example, a Welsh patriot might feel proud to be Welsh and love their country`s culture and values, but still be happy to be a part of the United Kingdom. A Welsh nationalist might feel that Wales should be separate from the UK, and feel intolerant of people or things from outside their country.

Parliament

Parliament in the UK is different from the Government. Parliament dozen`t decide how to run the country, but does approve/change the country`s laws and review how the Government is spending our money.

Patriotism

Feeling love and devotion towards your country and its values/beliefs.

Assignments

Brainstorming

⇨ What is citizenship?

⇨ What is a 'global citizen'?

Research

⇨ Recently, over 20,000 people from 18 countries took part in a poll which discovered that more and more people now identify themselves as global citizens rather than citizens of their country. In pairs, create a questionnaire to find out whether people in your area feel this way. Distribute your questionnaire to family and friends then write a brief summary of your findings. Include graphs to demonstrate your results.

⇨ Research some local volunteering schemes in your area and choose one you find particularly interesting. Create a PowerPoint presentation about this scheme, aimed at persuading people to take part. Then perform your presentation for your class (it should be no more than three minutes long).

⇨ Research the BBC Radio 1 scheme '1 Million Hours' and write a summary of the scheme.

⇨ Research the role of the Monarch in the UK and write a short report that could feature in an online citizenship magazine.

Design

⇨ Choose an article from this book and create an illustration to accompany it.

⇨ Design a leaflet displaying the information from the article *Types of British nationality* on pages three–five. Use pictures to illustrate your leaflet and make sure information is clearly laid out. Also include some links people can visit for further information.

⇨ Design a poster that shows the top ten things you believe to be 'typically' or 'quintessentially' British.

⇨ Design a campaign to encourage people to join 'Asgardia' – the 'first nation state in space'. Think about the values people should share and what kind of identity you want to create for this nation. Your campaign should include a webpage and some posters.

⇨ Design a website aimed at young people (aged 14 and above), which explains 'Brexit'. Work in small groups and think about how you can make the information easy to understand.

Oral

⇨ Choose one of the illustrations from this book and, in pairs, discuss what you think the artist was trying to portray.

⇨ In small groups, discuss the concept of 'British identity'. What kinds of things make you 'feel' British? How important are each of the following:

- To have been born in Britain

- To have British citizenship

- To have lived in Britain for most of one's life

- To be able to speak English

- To be a Christian

- To respect Britain's political institutions and laws

- To feel British

- To have British ancestry.

Put these things in order of importance, and then share with the rest of your class.

⇨ Communities Secretary Sajid Javid has suggested that public office holders may have to pledge an oath to British values. This would include elected officials, civil servants and council workers. In pairs discuss whether you think this is a good idea and write a proposed pledge that could be used.

⇨ What does it mean to be a 'responsible citizen'? Discuss in pairs.

Reading/writing

⇨ Write definitions of the terms 'citizenship' and 'global citizen'.

⇨ Read the article *Naturalisation as a British citizen…* on page six then write a summary for your school newspaper.

⇨ Write a blog post explaining why it is important to feel a sense of 'regional' identity. Think about the region you live in, what is great about it? What is unique about it? Include these things in your blog post and read the article *Cornwall and Yorkshire show regional identities run deep in England, too* on page 11 if you need some inspiration.

⇨ What does it mean to be a citizen? Write 500 words exploring this question.

Acknowledgements

The publisher is grateful for permission to reproduce the material in this book. While every care has been taken to trace and acknowledge copyright, the publisher tenders its apology for any accidental infringement or where copyright has proved untraceable. The publisher would be pleased to come to a suitable arrangement in any such case with the rightful owner.

Images

All images courtesy of iStock except pages 10, 29 and 30 © Pixabay, page 14 © Meg Nielson and page 15 © NASA.

Icons

Icons on pages 40 & 41 made by Freepik from www.flaticon.com.

Illustrations

Don Hatcher: pages 1 & 24. Simon Kneebone: pages 20 & 27. Angelo Madrid: pages 6 & 28.

Additional acknowledgements

Editorial on behalf of Independence Educational Publishers by Cara Acred.

With thanks to the Independence team: Mary Chapman, Sandra Dennis, Jackie Staines and Jan Sunderland.

Cara Acred

Cambridge, September 2017